How To Eliminate Stress And Anxiety Through The Occult

Crystals, Gemstones, Meditation, Herbs, Oils, Visualization, Chakras, Music, Prayer, Mandalas, Mantras, Incense, Candles
AND MORE!

By María D' Andrea

HOW TO ELIMINATE STRESS AND ANXIETY THROUGH THE OCCULT

Crystals, Gemstones, Meditation, Herbs, Oils, Visualization, Chakras, Music, Prayer, Mandalas, Mantras, Incense Candles and more

By Maria D' Andrea

How To Eliminate Stress and Anxiety Through The Occult
Crystals, Gemstones, Meditation, Herbs, Oils, Visualization,
Chakras, Music, Prayer, Mandalas, Mantras, Incense Candles
and more

By Maria D' Andrea
© Copyright 2012 Global Communications

All Rights Reserved.
No part of this book may be reproduced, stored in a retrieval system, or transmitted, in any form or by any means, electronic, mechanical, photocopying, recording, or otherwise, without prior permission of the author and publisher. Manufactured in the United States.

Printed in the United States of America

Timothy Green Beckley: Editorial Director
Carol Ann Rodriguez: Publishers Assistant
Tim R. Swartz: Editor and Layout
Sean Casteel: Associate Editor
William Kern: Associate Editor
Cover Art By Carol Ann Rodriguez

For Free Subscription To The Conspiracy Journal Write:

Tim Beckley/Global Communications
Box 753, New Brunswick, NJ 08903

Sign Up On Line: MRUFO8@hotmail.com

www.ConspiracyJournal.Com

www.TeslasSecretLab.Com

OTHER BOOKS BY THE AUTHOR:

Heaven Sent Money Spells - Divinely Inspired For Your Wealth

Secret Occult Gallery And Spell Casting Formulary: A Psychic Insider's Personal Study Guide To Over 50 Rarely Discussed Occult Topics

Secret Magical Elixirs Of Life

Your Personal Mega Power Spells - For Love, Luck, Prosperity

Occult Grimoire And Magical Formulary: A Workbook For Creating A Positive Life

FOR SERVICES AND PRODUCTS CONTACT:

Maria D'Andrea MsD,D.D.,DRH
www.mariadandrea.com

Table of Contents

Dedication……………………………………………………… 1
Acknowledgements……………………………………….. 2
Forward……………………………………………………….. 3
Introduction………………………………………………….. 4
Chapter One……………………………………………………5
Chapter Two……………………………………………………9
Guided Meditation Is A Power Tool……………………10
Short Mediation Version………………………………….. 13
Chapter Three………………………………………………16
Chapter Four………………………………………………..20
Overcome Physical Mishaps And Injuries………………..22
Recreating Prosperity…………………………………………..24
Achieving Your Right Weight……………………………….27
Counteract Feeling Rushed………………………………….29
Reactivating Your Physical Movements ……………………31
Addictions……………………………………………………….32
How To Live In The Present Moment……………………34
Dealing With External Interruptions……………………...36
Creating Your Rhythm With Hectic Work………………38
Rediscovering Your Sexual Prowess……………………...40
Handle Changes With Career And Home………………..42
Chapter Five……………………………………………….46
Take Control Of Emotional Imbalances Or Moodiness………..47
Fidelity ……………………………………………………………48
Achieve Peace And Harmony In Personal Or Business Affairs…51
Dealing With Separation Of Spouse Or Romantic Partner…….53
How To Change How Others See You…………………… 54

Reclaim Your Sexual Drive..56
Rebuilding Self-Image...59
Erase Despair...62
Attract Fun, Friendship And Love.....................................64
How To Handle Unstable Kids And Disgruntled Workers........66
Mental Power And Focus..68
Change Lack Of Satisfaction..71
Counteract Unjust Treatment...73
Chapter Six...75
Chapter Seven... 79
Manifesting Quick Money.. 83
Chapter Eight.. 85
Meditation And Prayer... 85
De-Stress With Gemstone Meditation..............................89
Meditation With Herbal Applications...............................92
Ancient Oil Meditation... 94
Incense Meditation...95
Candles And Guided Meditation......................................97
Chapter Nine...100
Chapter Ten..125
Maria's Bio..136

How To Eliminate Stress And Anxiety Through The Occult

Dedication

To Rick Holecek, my son - whose multiple talents & psychic abilities enhance all of our lives.

To Rob D'Andrea, my son - who's an inspiration on how to be positive in life & for his ability to achieve.

To Gina Holecek, my daughter in-law - who combines her intelligence with helping others.

To Maria Berde, my mother - who has the spirit of exploration.

To my spiritual brother, Bishop Francis E. Revels-Bey – who has walked the Path of Light with me for many years.

To Jimmy Dar Conte – who is special to me for his creative ideas and energetic and loving support in completing this book.

To Lisa Sharvin, my friend – with her expertise in photography and makeup is always there to help.

To Timothy Beckley, my friend – who inspires me to always do better.

How To Eliminate Stress And Anxiety Through The Occult

Acknowledgements

Rob D'Andrea – my son, for doing the proof reading for this book and his support.

Rick Holecek – my son, for being enthusiastic about this book and contributing insightful ideas.

Bro. Francis Revels-Bey – for contributing his time and expertise to the completion of this book.

God blessed me in the form of having positive, spiritual people around me who contribute in unlimited ways to my life. I am very thankful for all of their motivation, input, support and love.

How To Eliminate Stress And Anxiety Through The Occult

Foreword

THIS is an exciting book from noted author Maria D'Andrea that will help every reader to learn how to handle and eliminate stress from their daily lives.

I have been involved in the fields of meditation, metaphysics and tai chi on both the professional and personal levels for over 30 years and find all the journeys in these meditations concise, informative and very valuable.

I urge everyone who reads this work to delve into the passion of self-discovery, balance and wholeness as your life will be surely enhanced on all levels.

Bishop Francis E. Revels-Bey

January 2012

New Mexico

How To Eliminate Stress And Anxiety Through The Occult

Introduction

THROUGHOUT the centuries, various techniques, remedies and formulae have been utilized to make lives more positive in all cultures.

Through this method, you can achieve harmony, balance and improve your way of life! You will be happier and more fulfilled when you have been able to control the stress that so many struggle with.

Stress creates problems in people's lives through unstable sleep patterns, intense jobs that raise blood pressure, long work hours that weaken the body and spirit, exposing them to imbalances of all kinds, improper diet, a hectic work schedule, headaches, relationship upsets, and feelings of being misunderstood, to name a few.

Turn negative stress around and life will become a positive experience for you.

Even though the meditations are serious and are able to help improve your life, remember to laugh. Laughter is one of the best methods to de-stress.

Utilize these powerful methods that I am giving you to take control and have a bright future.

Love & Light,
Maria

CHAPTER ONE

The Law of Meditation

THERE are numerous forms of mediation. In this book, we will center our attention on Stress Relief. Meditation is a pathway that you are on. The path connects physical reality to spiritual reality. Meditation is the link between the two realms – man and spirit, a direct line.

It is an ancient technique with the goal of achieving a higher state of consciousness. This allows confused, disconnected, stressed thoughts to fade and be replaced by a positive, controlled consciousness to manifest your intent/goals and to dispel negative life situations.

We are spiritual beings living in a physical body. We need to utilize both physical senses and psychic intuitive senses to create a balanced, prosperous, joyous, happy life. There are various methods to attain this.

Some meditation/concentration methods are: Prayer Beads, Tai Chi (considered a moving meditation); music; mantra; mandala; visual object focus; Whirling Dervish; Temple dancers; biofeedback; seed meditation; meditation for psychic/spiritual awareness and guided meditation.

For our purposes, the main form in this book is guided meditation. Guided meditation is a technique utilized by a spiritual teacher or person to bring you or a group to a state of quietude of your body, emotions and mind. Focus is narrowed to the spiritual teacher's direction in order to achieve a predetermined goal.

<u>The Law of Meditation</u> states that when a conscious mind, for a length of time, is focused on a point, the five physical senses are quieted. Thus, thoughts flow from Divine Power (God or whatever you choose to call your Source). When your consciousness is awake fully, you would not be receptive to this higher form of insight. Meditation is a conscious control for a time of your outer awareness.

Authors, scientists, musicians, poets, inventors, occultists, artists, among others, all have this ability. They become so focused on something that everything else seems to disappear.

Meditation gives your body (such as when dealing with health issues), your emotions and mind (stress, aggravation, fear, unworthiness, lack of confidence, etc.) a way to improve situations.

Knowing where you put your focus/your intent is very important. Wherever you put your intent, that is what you will attract to yourself. Thus, utilizing meditation to focus on what you want will cause you to have less negativity and more positive situations in your life.

Meditation tunes you into problem solving, intuitive insight (ex: where luck comes from), ideas, prosperity, success, relaxation, skill enhancement, decision making and a stress-free life.

Meditation has also been scientifically tested. It was discovered that body chemistry, the sympathetic nervous system and metabolism had a definite change. The mind, when speaking normally to people in a conscious state, has a brainwave tested to be on a Beta level. When in a meditative state, this level changes to Alpha or Theta waves.

You will learn how to turn your life around. You have the Law of Attraction at work. "Like attracts like" is a metaphysical statement. Each of us has an electromagnetic field. What it contains in thought (electromagnetic mental field), as well as in the physical, is what it attracts to us.

It is important to have a positive attitude, only do positive things in your life, act on the information you receive in meditation or on your meditation intent.

When you meditate over a period of time, you will see the benefits and results yourself. Work with the Law of Meditation. Gain control over your life. It is within your reach!

How To Eliminate Stress And Anxiety Through The Occult

CHAPTER TWO
How To Meditate

I have helped and taught meditation since I was sixteen. These guided meditations are my methods. I created them for various clients and situations. They work! They are power tools!

Meditation is a much misunderstood and underestimated tool. It gives you the ability to tune into a Higher Source and into your Higher Consciousness. It is a direct line to guidance, direction, spiritual awareness and intuition.

It can give immediate benefits. Follow these methods. Situations in your life are about to change for you!

It is very important to FIRST use a form of Spiritual Protection prior to beginning meditation.

You also need to either tape record the meditation or if you have a good memory, read it and then mentally focus on it with your eyes closed. If you record it, you will not have to think about what comes next and can relax and go easily through the guided meditations when you are ready. Record the protection, relaxation process and guided meditation of your choice with a slow, steady voice.

<u>Guided Meditation Is A Power Tool</u>

In the following meditations for various intents, remember to always start at the following point:

"Beginning Meditation"

Find a quiet area where you will not be disturbed. Shut the phone off. Loosen tight clothing, so it will not be a distraction.

Find a comfortable position for your body in an arm chair. In this manner, your subconscious mind will not be worried about being too relaxed and falling off the chair. Otherwise, your body will become uncomfortable and thus bring you out of the meditation.

As you <u>sit in a chair,</u> elevate your feet a little, such as on a pillow. Think of it as an antenna. You do not want to "ground" yourself. <u>DO NOT cross any part of your body</u> (such as crossing your arms or legs). You do not want to block the energy flow. Later, once you get the feel, you can meditate anywhere and not worry about your feet being off the ground. But for now, do it full power.

<u>Close your eyes.</u>

<u>Relax your body.</u> You can use the progressive relaxation method:

1. Sit with the spine erect, feet flat on the floor and begin breathing deeply and evenly with your eyes closed. Continue to do this throughout the exercise.

How To Eliminate Stress And Anxiety Through The Occult

2. Relax
- TOES, then
- ARCHES OF FEET, then
- RISING TO ANKLES
- UPWARD TO CALVES
- TO KNEES
- TO UPPER LEGS
- TO THIGHS AND HIPS
- TO SMALL OF BACK
- RISING UP THE SPINE
- TO NECK AND SHOULDERS
- MOVING DOWNWARD TO THE UPPER ARMS AND TO THE FOREARMS
- TO WRISTS, HANDS AND FINGERS
- BACK UP THE ARMS TO THE SHOULDERS
- THEN MOVING DOWNWARD THROUGH THE CHEST AND STOMACH
- AGAIN MOVING UPWARD TO THE NECK (making it loose and LIMP)
- ALLOWING THE RELAXATION TO MOVE TO THE SCALP
- MOVING OVER FOREHEAD AND BROW (relaxing as it goes)
- DOWN TO THE EYES
- NOW SQUEEZE THE EYES AS HARD AS YOU CAN

- NOW RELAX THEM AND FEEL ALL THE PEACEFULLNESS AND RELAXING POWER FLOW OVER THEM
- ALLOW THAT RELAXATION TO MOVE TO THE CHEEKS AND JAW
- NOW ALLOW A SMALL SPACE BETWEEN YOUR TEETH SO THAT YOUR JAW CAN REMAIN SLACK

Let yourself <u>feel positive</u>, happy, competent. Whatever you feel as positive (not the time to think of your bills).

Next, do <u>abdominal breathing</u>. It is deep breathing. When you take a breath in, your stomach expands out. When you let your breath out, your stomach pulls in.

Do this for a little while. Then with each, count backwards from ten to one. At the end you should have a very relaxed, "up" feeling.

Then place your focus on your <u>Third Eye</u>. This is in the middle of your forehead. Visualize a screen, any type. In white (if you do not see white, try golden or yellow). Such as a T.V. screen, or movie or drive-in movie screen.

<u>Wait</u> a few seconds.

Now, you are ready to proceed with your meditation techniques. From here, they change according to what you pick as your meditation purpose.

- Prior to each meditation, refer back to this "Beginning Meditation" stage -

When you are ready to stop, simply decide to do so. Otherwise, when done, you may come out of it automatically.

When you are finished, open your eyes slowly and take your time getting up. Sometimes you will feel so relaxed, it will be difficult to jump up and run around. Give your body time to get back to its normal, everyday energy levels.

The last step is written under "For Both Forms."

Once you have gone through the relaxation method numerous times, you may feel you can move on to relaxing quicker. If you are at that point, try the following technique. If it does not work as well for you, go back to the longer version.

SHORT MEDIATION VERSION

- Sit as before.
- Do your Protection first.
- Close your eyes.
- Tighten all your muscles for a few seconds, then relax.
- Take a few deep breaths.
- Focus on your breathing being slow and natural.
- Relax more and more with each breath.

- Take your time.

- Now focus your attention on the space where your third eye is located (in the middle of your forehead).

- Then focus a little above that and in front of you. You will "see" a blank space, gray, white, or a color. Try to visualize a white or golden-white space.

For Both Forms

At the end of both meditation methods, you need to remember to close down after each meditation session.

Before you start doing other things, as the <u>last step – CLOSE YOUR AURA!</u>

To do this, hold your arms at shoulder level at your sides, then cross them over your chest. Cross your legs. You need to "pull in" your energy body, since you were just very "open." Otherwise you may get fall-out. Example: being emotionally too sensitive.

<u>Remember</u> to go through all the steps leading to the guided meditation you picked and the ending technique. This will give you the full benefits.

These methods are your tools to positive transformation. Utilize them often. You can do it!

How To Eliminate Stress And Anxiety Through The Occult

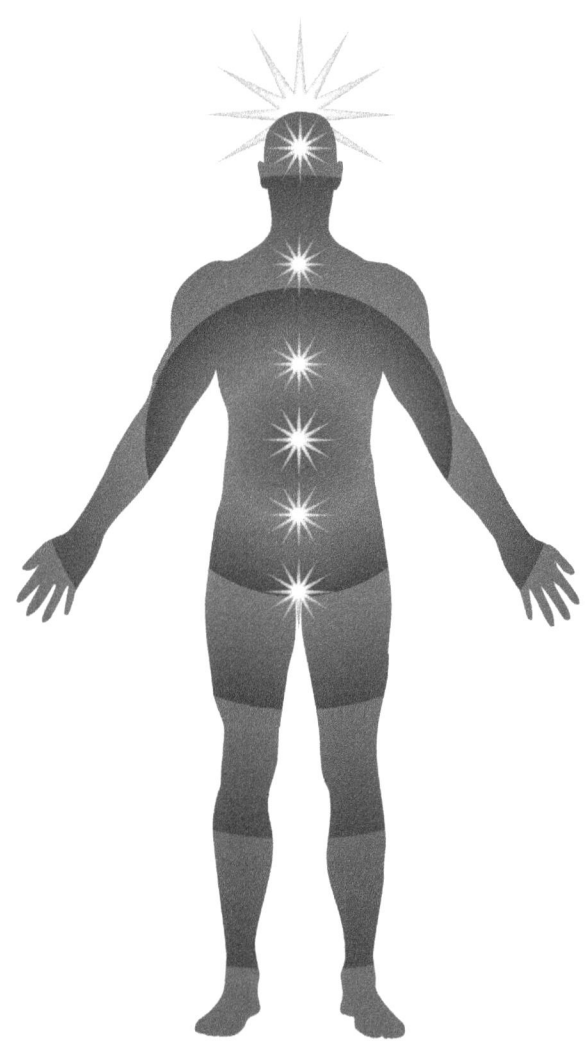

CHAPTER THREE
Spiritual Protection

SPIRITUAL Protection is a SURVIVAL TOOL!

When you are in a meditative state, an alpha/theta brainwave level, you are very open to suggestion, the spirit plane, positive and negative energies.

You need to be safe first. To have your mind, body and spirit always only open to positive energies. After all, if you tune into a negative information source, how can you be accurate? Also, you need to be "safe" <u>any</u> time you are open psychically.

If you have a protection method that works for you, continue to use it. Do so <u>prior</u> to meditation.

If you do not have a method, utilize the prayer I created specifically for this purpose. Depending on your belief system, substitute your own word for God/Divine Power where needed.

Know in your heart that all protection comes from Divine Power. As soon as you ask, it is done.

> ### Protection Power
>
> ### By Rev. Maria D'Andrea
>
> **As above, so below. I acknowledge Divine Power _is_ my Source.**
>
> **I am NOW protected from all negativity through the Power of God. Nothing can harm me on any level. Through Divine Power, nothing can hurt my mind, body or soul. As I think this, I know it. So Be It !**
>
> **Thank you God.**

Remember, the Bible in Job 11:18 said, "God will protect you and give you rest."

Spiritual protection, also known as Psychic Self-Defense, is a powerful weapon. There are many forms and tools utilized. It would be a book by itself, so we do not need to go into the subject more. I teach classes on this and various other interests in the psychic and metaphysical fields.

I find that when you work with any energies, such as meditation, where you are more open to vibrational and spiritual influences, you <u>always</u> need to protect yourself. I can only point this out, but you need to be the one to implement it.

Use spiritual protection whenever you feel you need it, as well as for meditation.

How To Eliminate Stress And Anxiety Through The Occult

CHAPTER FOUR

Guided Meditations To Eliminate Physical And Mental Stress

THESE meditations will help you to gain control and cancel disturbances and negative situations in your life stemming from physical or mental situations.

You need to balance and counteract situations such as: drugs, sexual problems, lack of a job or money, balancing a hectic work schedule (which can affect blood pressure), weight, etc.

When you are in harmony within yourself, your life will improve and move forward.

Stress influences your body and mind to various degrees. Most of our problems can be traced back to stress being the cause – whether physically, mentally, spiritually, emotionally, or a combination of these.

We all respond in various ways to the world as we perceive it. Whether we respond in a positive or negative way to outward stimuli depends on our outlook and life experiences.

We can consciously change and improve situations by utilizing guided meditation to direct positive transformations to build a better life.

What we focus on expands our lives. Our focus is positive, exciting, unlimited and empowering in meditation.

How To Eliminate Stress And Anxiety Through The Occult

Physical and mental limitations which caused stress within ourselves or from others can be cancelled. Make changes in your life through these meditation sessions to bring success and happiness to yourself.

Stress is a state that manifests due to a variety of reasons, such as financial problems or a change in relocation of your home or job. It manifests on the physical plane in many ways. To bring balance, we get rid of stress so it influences you in a positive way, to transform ulcers, trigger abdominal muscles to relax, align hormonal imbalances, to bring harmony, bring muscle tension to tranquility, and to increase the blood's oxygen level, to name a few.

Mentally, people who are in professions which involve deadlines, taking risks or making complex personal decisions are in need of stress reduction. Feeling there's a lack of time or too many distractions, like the radio, TV, etc. can be affected to create a positive change.

Overall, stress is one of the most frequent root causes of problems with humanity as a whole.

Some stress is needed and is a positive survival instinct. We want to influence the negative, constant stress to be changed by utilizing guided meditation as a tool.

Nothing can hold you back or slow you down from achieving your focused positive goals.

Choose the guided meditation that fits your circumstance and alter your life!

Overcome Physical Mishaps And Injuries
Meditation:
(before starting refer back to the Beginning Meditation)

With eyes closed, picture a serene countryside. See beautiful yellow sunflowers and rusty-colored mums waving slowly in the soft breeze. Beyond them, you see a blue lagoon.

Now, see, in front of you, a brown dirt path. Start walking on the path, which will take you to the lagoon.

As you walk steadily and happily, notice that you feel peaceful and serene. You hear soft peaceful music in the air all around you. It does not matter what the source of this beautiful soft music is, just that it is uplifting and makes you feel good.

Take your time walking until you get to the lagoon.

As you see the lagoon's edge, you notice a square shaped treasure box on the edge of the water.

Go there and sit next to it, on the flat ground.

You know instinctively this box is meant for you. You feel happy and excited that you found it.

You look at your surroundings and notice the blue wavy water. There are sunflowers nearby the water. The music is still soft in the background. You are sitting comfortably in front of the treasure box.

Focus your attention back on the box again. Notice that the box is unlocked. Slowly open the box, which is filled with gems and stones.

As you look at all the stones and gems, you notice a rust colored polished stone called jasper and another stone called turquoise, the stone that gives this color its name.

You pick them up and instantly feel surrounded by green and orange light. You feel perfectly healthy and vibrant. You are bathed in the lights as you hold onto the stones.

You put your hand into the blue water holding onto the stones. You let the water flow over your hand and all your pain and all situations connected to any accident drain from you – emotionally, physically, mentally and spiritually into the water.

Leave your hand comfortably in the water until all forms of negativity drain away.

Feel relaxed, uplifted, joyous, comfortable and serene.

Know that these stones help you with your situation. See your situation flowing away to leave room for all that is positive.

Take your hand out of the water with the stones. Put the stones into your pocket. The green and orange colored lights will stay and surround you until all is perfectly well and resolved.

Close the box and look around once more. Take your time.

Stand up and slowly walk past the flowers, back to where you started.

Remember all that has occurred. Know that you can come back here at any time you choose.

Relax and take a few deep breaths. Feel happy and in charge of yourself. Then slowly open your eyes.

Do not move quickly getting up.

Recreating Prosperity

Meditation:
(before starting refer back to the Beginning Meditation)

Keeping your eyes closed, visualize yourself on a flat plateau overlooking the desert. You see cacti and other vegetation. It feels very peaceful and majestic.

Turn around to see the entry to a large cave.

It looks inviting to you and you know you have come to this plateau seeking this cave.

You feel happy, elated and curious about the cave.

You walk forward at a leisurely pace.

You notice the walls are lit. Oil lamps are attached to the walls on both sides.

You walk slowly toward your goal, which you

know is somewhere in the cave.

As you walk, you touch one of the walls and feel the smooth surface.

You see an opening in front of you as the cave entryway opens into a large cave.

In the middle of the cave, there is an altar about three feet high.

You walk up to it. There, on top of the altar, is a clay tablet. As you look at the tablet, you see bright gold writing.

The tablet is meant for you and tells you about your future.

As you read, it tells you that all which you desire comes to you NOW! Focus on getting money, abundance, prosperity and/or the "perfect" job. Be persistent in your focus. See yourself in a room with money all around you everywhere. Your pockets are overflowing with large bills. Know that all your needs are met and more. You have more than you need. This comes from your perfect job. If one job does not come in, another one will. The one that is perfect for you.

Relax, knowing your perfect job and financial abundance are being made manifest NOW.

Daily focus on "knowing" you're safe and taken care of by Higher Spiritual Forces. Divine Power is always there as your Source. Always there to open a door for you when you need it.

How To Eliminate Stress And Anxiety Through The Occult

Trust in the Higher Power and go about your daily life happy in the knowledge that the perfect job/money is coming to you.

The tablet was written specifically for you to find in this mystical cave. The prophecy of your bright future is yours. Even if it comes to you at the last minute, it still comes to you on time.

Relax, knowing this information to be accurate for your life.

Now look up at the cave's ceiling and all around the walls. As you look, it begins to glow with golden light. As it brightens, you notice that there are billions of gold pieces embedded in the cave walls and ceiling. As you look down, you see gold scattered around the floor.

You realize you could take all of it with you. However, you know that you have more than enough money coming to you and decide you do not need the gold you found here. After all, you definitely have abundance and prosperity coming to you.

You now know this, feel this, see it happening and trust in the tablets information for you.

You turn around and go slowly back to the cave's entrance.

As you emerge into the sunlight, you feel relaxed, happy and with a strong sense of expectancy.

The feeling will stay with you as you go about your daily business.

Take a few slow, deep breaths and slowly open your eyes.

Be aware of your positive feelings and focus on them whenever you need to.

ACHIEVING YOUR RIGHT WEIGHT
Meditation:
(before starting refer back to the Beginning Meditation)

You are relaxed and comfortable. With your eyes closed, envision yourself at the entrance to a museum.

You see a large, wooden door in front of you, with a decorative metal doorknob. There are two great dragons standing guard. One represents your "will" to accomplish your goal. The other represents your emotional drive to gain your desires. Reach for it and open the door.

There, in front of you, is a well-lit hallway. The wooden floors gleam with polish. The white walls seem to softly glow. You feel strong, vibrant and interested.

As you walk along the hallway, you notice pictures on the walls on both sides of you. You take your time and look. Look at the one to your right. What is it? People, scenery, animals? What colors?

As you walk, you notice that at the end of the hallway, there is a pedestal with soft lights shining on it. You cannot make out what is on it yet, due to the lights.

As you get closer, you see a statue of yourself

exactly as you imagine your "Perfect" self to be.

Take your time and walk around the statue. Look at every angle. Notice everything, such as: hair-color, hair length and style, your body shape, height, coloring, etc.

Note that this is your Higher Self. This is truly you. Since it is you, it is easy to achieve this effect in your daily life.

Look at the statue of your "Perfect" self. Notice that there are wooden steps leading to the statue. Walk up the steps and into the statue itself. You become one with it. Look through the eyes. Move your "Perfect" body. Become aware of how you feel. You are lighter and happier. Consciously become aware of your body and how it moves and looks. Know that this look is what you are and can achieve.

After you are finished, step out of your "Perfect" self and down the steps. Take your time and look at "yourself" on the pedestal from all angles.

You already felt what it is like to be your "Perfect" self, so it will be easy and effortless to achieve your goal. Your goal to become the person you desire to be.

Walk back down the hallway, taking your time. Go to the front door, open it and slowly open your eyes.

You may do this meditation once a day to re-affirm your goal. Do it as frequently as you wish. Keep focused on a picture of your "Perfect" self.

Breathe slowly and open your eyes.

COUNTERACT FEELING RUSHED
Meditation:
(before starting refer back to the Beginning Meditation)

See a picture of a sunny green pasture with a white path in front of you winding through it.

See yourself stepping onto the path and slowly, lazily, strolling along it. Take your time to see the plants or flowers as you pass. Examine them. Look at the colors and the shades. Are they in sunlight or shade? Do they cast shadows? Lean down and touch some of them. How do they feel? Soft, velvety, stiff, firm? Pay attention to the feelings. Do you see friendly animals or birds? Where are they? What do they look like? What are they doing? Can you hear them? Look at them with all your senses and look at details. Take your time.

When you are finished examining your surroundings, start walking on the white path once more. You will see a serene blue lake. Walk to the edge, where you will sit on the ground. Let your fingers slowly move the water back and forth. Be aware of the feeling, color and smell of the water.

Look into the water and into the depths, see various clocks floating slowly on the undercurrents.

Notice that, in the distance, along the right shoreline, the lake empties slightly into a stream.

All the clocks slowly float toward and down the

stream. It is relaxing, comforting. You feel good about time moving slowly and at a comfortable pace.

Look back at the serene water. Reflected back, you see yourself looking peaceful, calm, relaxed and smiling. The water reflects your happy mood. Smile as you become aware of how good you feel. Be aware of having enough time for everything you need to do, with a feeling of moving at a comfortable pace. You always have more than enough time for everything. Easily. Happily. Focus on this for a moment.

Take your time to let various happy thoughts cross your mind.

When you are finished, be aware of how wonderful and relaxed you feel. Know that you can come back to this spot at any time you wish.

Slowly, get up and retrace your steps to where you started on the white path.

Look around you once more. Know that you will feel relaxed, happy and calm as you move throughout your day.

Remember, you always have more than enough time to do all that you wish. You have time and more to spare, to do everything at a comfortable pace.

Smile and feel the relaxation. It will stay with you as you move throughout the day.

Take a deep breath and very slowly open your eyes. When you are ready, get up slowly and go about your day.

On and off, when you wish to, simply recall the lake and how you felt.

Reactivating Your Physical Movements

Meditation:
(before starting refer back to the Beginning Meditation)

Relax, breathe gently and deeply. Imagine you are at an amusement theme park of your choice. You are in search of inner joy, energy, fun and excitement. You feel yourself drawn to a water slide.

As you arrive, it's your turn to get prepared for your ride. Your rhythmic breathing massages your mind and body, further relaxing you, for the ride is now before you.

You climb into the cool water and begin your wild ride. You descend with water gushing up and cushioning your ride. It playfully splashes your face and body. With each twisting and winding path, memories of an active, playful childlike atmosphere return to the truer essence of your being.

You are aware that everyone around you is having as much fun as you. The water gently dissolves your fears, lethargy and lack of energy. Each turn is more surprising and exhilarating than the last one.

All that was boring and bothersome no longer is disturbing to you. You are allowing yourself to flow like water, offering no resistance. The only shape is not having a shape. The water is inviting, active and playful. You are totally involved – dancing with the excitement and pleasures of life. You are the energy of life.

You are happy and active, reminding you of children. You remember how difficult it was to sit in one spot for too long and not fidget. You regain this same excited feeling. Fun and joy become part of your life once more.

You gently splash into the pool of water at the bottom of the slide.

You feel exhilarated and full of energy. You cannot stand still. You are looking forward to going back on the line for another ride.

You come out of the water and know these feelings are the true you. The you as a child and one that is you now.

Take three breaths and open your eyes.

After a few minutes, get up and start doing things. Make a plan for fun, activity, joy and laughter.

ADDICTIONS

Meditation:
(before starting refer back to the Beginning Meditation)

With eyes closed, visualize yourself floating downstream on a river. You see beautiful scenes and you realize that you are heading straight into a large water fountain filled with colorful bubbly foam and a rainbow of immense joy, inner peace and love.

A big splash is made as you land and find yourself floating in a sea of love and excitement. Keep breathing deeply and gently for a moment.

The water is comfortable and cleanses away all feelings that are not positive, happy or supportive.

All that has gone before in your life is over. It is no longer part of who you are. It is un-changeable. It is a finished chapter in your life.

Yet, as a unique human, you know we are capable of unlimited success, happiness and achievement.

As you float in the water, you see all kinds of colors and lights. You feel the water surround you and buoy you up. You are having fun. You do not need to think past this joy, just enjoy it.

The playful water tickles your toes. You splash about in excitement.

Everything negative has cleansed away.

You can enjoy your life now and set new goals.

Take your time. One goal at a time is fine. It is relaxing, unrushed, uplifting and successful.

Set your sights high, knowing you can accomplish anything.

After all, you are a spiritual being. Spiritual beings

are always without limits. We just forget that at times. You know this now and will remember.

You splash around and bob up and down. Have fun and laugh as the water rolls over your legs. Life is becoming fun, as it was meant to be. You are getting excited at all the plans you can make and achieve.

Your future is being planned by YOU NOW. Whatever wonderful plans you can think up, you know you can do.

Look at what makes your life fun, happy and enjoyable.

Flow gently and happily for a moment. Smile at your thoughts.

Let yourself slowly come back as you retain the memory of love and life being fun again.

Open your eyes. SMILE........

How To Live In The Present Moment
Meditation:
(before starting refer back to the Beginning Meditation)

Now is the time for you to imagine that you are a stately noble tree. You are the tallest one around. You begin – let yourself start to feel as though your legs and feet extend deeply into the mountain. You can feel the current of Earth energy swirl up your feet and legs – right up to your pelvis. You are feeling firm yet flexible.

You are becoming more than a tree as your breath

grows deeper with its own rhythmic flow. As the Light of Earth moves upward, you feel the essence of tree energy flow down into the Earth. Both energies blend and swirl through and around you. Feel the mind relax and open. All stagnation, anxiety and frailty leave your body. You quickly become filled with new purpose and strength to overcome any obstacle.

You look at the present and feel elated. There is nothing that you cannot handle. You enjoy the moment, the day and night. Today, you get to do whatever you feel.

You can communicate your thoughts and feelings. You can share a lunch break. You can go and spend the night stargazing. Think of all the possibilities. Make a mental list.

What can you do today that makes you or someone else feel good? Start with just one thing.

Remember it later and do it. Each day holds its own potential. Its own unlimited possibilities.

You are just as the tree: Roots from your past make you who you are today; leaves and branches stretch toward tomorrow as your mind stretches to plan and expand your future; yet you are grounded in TODAY and in who you are to be stable, knowing that what you do today effects your future.

You look forward to planning each day as it happens.

You feel the oneness of the tree and Earth meeting

deeply in your heart, mind and body.

Relax and open your eyes to a great day.

Dealing With External Interruptions
Meditation:
(before starting refer back to the Beginning Meditation)

As your eyes close and you clear your mind, take a slow deep breath.

Envision yourself in the tropics, sitting under a palm tree with your back resting against the trunk.

You feel the sandy earth beneath you, the warm breeze enveloping you and the sunny sky above you.

You are relaxed and looking at the hills in the distance.

You see a bamboo hut to your right, just a few feet away. It has a colorful cotton fabric as the door. The hut interests you and peaks your curiosity.

You leisurely stand up and stroll to it.

The hut seems to be empty, yet there is the warm glow of a light from within.

You pull aside the curtain and see a large, flat, square piece of wood. It has carvings of ancient symbols around the edges, representing a powerful and strong God. The center of the square looks empty, yet glows from an unknown source. There are two pillars in front of it. One to the right and one to the left.

As you look at these ancient symbols, you can feel the energy of the Earth flowing around and through you.

The blank space within the symbols on the square begins to glow with a stronger light. It keeps your attention focused only on the center. You feel safe, comfortable and interested.

As you watch, it reminds you of a TV screen. You now look at it with all your focus and enthusiasm. You wonder what will happen next.

You instinctively feel that any question you ask will be given an answer.

You think for a moment of what you are working on that needs your full attention. As you decide on what that is, you ask for a solution or information about it.

Watching the screen, it turns a little brighter and starts showing you all kinds of information connected to your question.

You are relaxed and intrigued by this and cannot take your eyes off it.

You let it run its course and add a question about the subject here and there.

When it is all finished, the light grows dimmer and softer.

You have discovered a fantastic, unexplainable device. You close the curtain and go back to your comfortable seat beneath the palm. You sit down.

You spend some time reflecting on all the

information you received.

You realize that when you get curious or excited about anything, it holds your complete attention. You now know that you can regain this feeling about anything you choose.

Relaxed, comfortable and happy in your new ability, you smile and slowly open your eyes.

CREATING YOUR RHYTHM WITH HECTIC WORK
Meditation:
(before starting refer back to the Beginning Meditation)

Now it is time to slowly breathe, drop your shoulders and straighten your spine. Keep your eyes closed. The lids feel very heavy and relaxed.

Everyone can use some pleasure and excitement in their lives. Now is your time.

Picture an open entrance to a large four-sided pyramid in front of you.

It has a warm, welcoming feeling about it. You feel safe and relaxed.

You walk up to the entrance and look within. You see the flicker of numerous torches on the walls. They give warmth to the large room. You enter and stand in the center.

Slowly you turn and look in all directions. You notice a large metal scale against one wall. You walk to it and notice two plaques with writing at the foot of the scale. One plaque states – Place all your stress, worries, things yet to be done and all energy-draining things on this side of the scale. The other plaque states – Place all your joy, happiness, feelings of contentment and all other uplifting and positive things on this side of the scale.

You step back a few feet and contemplate the information. After all, it is ancient wisdom and knowledge that created this spectacular scale.

You decide to try it out. On one side, you start putting all the things you need to get done. You add them on, one by one. Think of all you need to do tomorrow. Add those on. Take your time and put everything on that belongs on this side.

Now, look at the other empty side. Go up to it and add on all the things you need to do to bring joy, harmony, happiness and positive things into your life. Look at what you can add on for tomorrow. Once again, take your time.

When you are finished, step back and look at the scale. You notice that the side with the energy- draining things is much heavier than the other side.

You are a little surprised to see such a big difference.

Start to think of how to balance the scale. Go to the heavy side and decide what is not needed at this time. Take it off and put it to the side in a metal pot labeled – EVENTUALLY.

Look at each situation one at a time and remove everything you can until the scale is almost balanced.

Now, go to the other side and add on things to make you happy until the scales are equal.

As you step back, you realize they are exactly aligned. You are overcome with happiness. Self-confident in the knowledge that all will be taken care of in its own time and that your life regained its balance, peace and harmony. You can relax, smile and know you can time what to do and when. You move through life easily and effortlessly, with your life under your own control.

You feel excited with higher energy than you had before.

You turn and walk back to the entrance. Each time you feel the need, come back to the pyramid to re-align.

Remember to keep the scale balanced. Feeling good and relaxed, open your eyes.

Rediscovering Your Sexual Prowess

Meditation:
(before starting refer back to the Beginning Meditation)

As your breath moves throughout your body, comfortably leave your eyes closed.

See yourself in a large glass building with metal frames. You are sitting in a cool, chrome armchair relaxing. You see everyone outside through the glass walls, running around and laughing. You are a comfortable observer.

As you watch, you start to feel more and more restless.

You wonder what they are saying, what they are laughing about. You start thinking about joining them. But you are so comfortable and adjusted to simply not participating.

As the day goes on, your restlessness increases. Your curiosity and sense of fun is increasing.

You make your decision. You decide to become part of the joy and excitement.

Walking to the glass door, you decide you have made the right decision for you. You push the door open. As you do so, you feel a surge of energy flow through you. You feel vibrantly alive. Every cell of your body is active. You feel the warmth of the Sun on your skin. You enjoy this feeling.

People come up to you and ask you to join them. You look at what different people are doing to be active.

Now, you pick an activity that you like and join that group.

Everyone else says you can join them later, if you wish.

You enjoy yourself immensely. You are an energetic, active, strong and exciting person. You notice that the opposite sex is very attracted to you. You feel confident and happy. You are full of energy and vitality.

You have fun and join in various activities, as you choose which to participate in.

You look at the glass building. It is beautiful, but you know that you have outgrown living there. You are not going back. You love this safe, emotional fast pace. You are safe and comfortable with these new people.

Your life is fun, energetic and better. You have put fun back by making the choice. You know it is the right one for you. You love the rays of the Sun warming you and energizing you to move on to greater experiences.

As you feel loving toward others, open your heart and safely let them in. Enjoy yourself, breathe deeply and open your eyes.

Handle Changes With Career And Home
Meditation:
(before starting refer back to the Beginning Meditation)

As you breathe deeply, focus on your muscles relaxing. Be comfortable.

Envision yourself standing on a mountaintop. There are trees all around and a vibrantly green clearing. You are in a mystical realm.

You approach the clearing and see a giant red dragon comfortably asleep. You recognize this dragon as an old friend. You have not seen each other for a long time. So you look forward to catching up on all the changes in both your lives since your last encounter.

You walk up to your friend. With a pat, you awaken the dragon.

Your friend is very happy to see you. You build a campfire and sit down on the ground. You both exchange stories for many comfortable, interesting hours.

You tell your old friend about how you are making vast changes in your life. However, you are unsure of obstacles and difficulties that might arise.

The dragon knows just what to do. At your friend's suggestion, you climb up onto his bright red back and hold on.

As he lifts into the clear silvery sky, you hang on.

As this is a mystical land, your destinations come up one at a time representing all of the potential blocks in life that can get in your way. You want the transition in your life to be smooth, effortless and fun. It is best to get rid of the blocks NOW.

As you soar to the first destination (situation) that might make this change difficult, you look down and see the block. Look at it closely and from all angles. Fly all around it. See what it truly is and then talk to your dragon. Come up with a solution. Discuss it. What will make this situation positive or dissolved? How can you handle it if it comes up?

Once decided and armed with solutions, the dragon flies higher. It shoots flames down on your block and dissolves it completely.

Now, move on to the next block and do the same things. Do this until all the blocks have disappeared in flames.

Once you are finished, look back and see the flames from the blocks being dispersed.

Know that your friend has helped to dissolve all that can be in your way.

You are now free to enjoy the changes in your life. After all, to live is to be in constant change and growth. It is something that you now look forward to with excitement, joy and expectancy.

As you circle and land, you feel lighter and happier. You look forward to all aspects of your life.

You climb down from the dragon's back and thank him for all his help.

As you say your goodbyes, you know you will be seeing each other again.

Walk back to where you started on the mountain.

Feel relaxed, happy and excited to begin your next journey in your life. Take your time and open your eyes.

How To Eliminate Stress And Anxiety Through The Occult

CHAPTER FIVE
Guided Meditations To Eliminate Emotional And Destructive Stress

IF you have read this far, then you have chosen to take advantage of these methods to bring success, balance and joy to your everyday life.

These meditations help you to gain peace, psychic awareness, love, friendship, self-confidence, energy, courage, strength, safety and stability, to name a few.

Guided meditations give you the focus and control to improve your life. The following meditations cover areas where you can transform situations to your benefit.

Focus, be calm and relaxed and open to inspiration, insight and positive changes to take place. Know it! Expect it! Allow Light to come into your life and banish the darkness.

God and the Universe have incredible power and force. It is non-limited. Through these meditations, you are tuning into this Source of Power. Utilize it, become One with it. Know that the only limitations you have are the ones you set yourself. Let go of these and allow the guided meditations to create your new success.

Your emotional state has an overall affect on your life. Let this be a positive one.

Let irritability, anxiety, frustration and fear dissipate and happiness permeate throughout your being.

Invoke joy, serenity, balance, calm and peace.

Know that anytime you wish, you can go back to the same guided mediation place. Do so once or as often as you feel. Your past is behind you. You can make changes in your present to create the future you choose. Do so now. There is a saying – Go Forward, God Has Your Back. God is always with you. You cannot go wrong when Divine Power is with you. Remember, as part of God, you not only have power, Y-O-U are power! Utilize it!

These meditations will guide you on the Path to eliminate obstacles and blocks.

Take Control Of Emotional Imbalances Or Moodiness

Meditation:
(before starting refer back to the Beginning Meditation)

Take several deep breaths to establish a nice rhythmic flow. Feel comfortable.

Begin to visualize yourself walking into a forest to regain calmness.

Notice the various shades of green leaves, the wide variety of texture of the bark on the trees, as well as the height of the trees themselves.

You notice that each tree has its own distinctive character. Soon you find yourself prepared to exchange energies. Place your palms on the trunk of a tree. You seek to find out all that you can by absorbing the tree's energy. Its tree energy nourishes you mentally by lending clarity of mind and organizes your thought processes.

It has a cooling effect that begins to help you to relax. As you do, you realize that you are able to feel yourself at one with Mother Earth.

Relax now and move your palms away from the tree, still keeping the energy connection.

The deep comfort that you receive rebuilds your emotional strength and aligns your spirit. You begin to do light stretching that allows the energy to extend into every part of your body.

Before you know it, you feel renewed and refreshed with peace of mind.

You let the energies flow back and forth between you and the tree.

Stay aware of your connection to your environment and breathe slowly and rhythmically. Take your time. Take a slow, deep breath and open your eyes.

FIDELITY

Meditation: (before starting refer back to the Beginning Meditation)

As you close your eyes and breathe deeply, focus on a large beige boulder underneath your feet.

Feel the chi, the energy of the boulder. Feel the steadiness and firmness. The solid, stable boulder is your Rock of Ages, the boulder that houses those qualities, just as Divine Power is there for you with the same qualities.

Allow this energy to flow up through the soles of your feet and permeate throughout your being.

You are the boulder.

Now, think of the situation with your partner. Ask yourself if the situation definitely exists. Then wait a few seconds until you feel an answer. You may feel that your partner is or is not cheating; hear the words or see a picture that tells you either way. You may need to repeat the question. Pay attention and keep open to an answer.

If your answer says "Yes," focus on how you feel. Angry, hurt, upset, calm or whatever your emotions are. Acknowledge your true feelings.

Pull the energy of the boulder up into your body. It gives you inner strength, Spiritual Power and stability to handle all that you need to handle.

Pull the energy from above you down through your crown chakra at the top of your head. This is the energy of Divine Power, of Higher Consciousness.

It also brings you stability, a link to your Spiritual Power and inner strength.

How To Eliminate Stress And Anxiety Through The Occult

Allow these energies to flow into you and meet in your solar plexus, about one hand width above your navel.

Extend your arms in front of you, aiming at Mother Earth. Send all negative feelings through your fingers into the ground. Cleanse yourself of all negativity. Shoot the energy through your fingers to ground them.

As you let go of the draining feelings, stop pulling your energy up from the boulder. Allow the positive energies from above to flow down through your crown chakra, directly into the boulder and then through it into the core of the Earth. There, let your energy, in strands, wrap around the core to hold and stabilize you there.

No matter what happens around you, know that you are grounded, stable and powerful. You are a child of Divine Power. You are a powerful being. The situation is not your problem; it is your partner's.

Focus on knowing that you have the right positive partner for you. Keep that focus and it will happen. Either "see" your partner in a positive situation with you or see a new partner being with you in a positive way.

Know that no matter what happens, you are stable, strong, you are free to do what you will, you are a positive Spiritual being. This is only a setback. A stepping stone. Focus on your boulder energy and know all will get resolved.

Pull all the energy into your body and contain it there. It stays with you to use, as you need it at all times.

Take a few deep breaths and slowly let your eyes open.

Feel your own self-assuredness.

ACHIEVE PEACE AND HARMONY IN PERSONAL OR BUSINESS AFFAIRS

Meditation:
(before starting refer back to the Beginning Meditation)

With your eyes closed, visualize the people who are difficult in your life, standing at a distance in front of you.

See them surrounded by walls of flame, reaching higher and higher.

Look at each person, one at a time. As you do so, take your time. Look at the person and focus on what makes it difficult to deal with this individual. Is it that he/she loves to argue, that this person never listens, or has a quality that goes against your ethics? Really look at the annoyance. Now, look at the person's personality. Is the hard time you are having with the individual personal or not?

Ask if there is anything you can do to change the situation. Then wait to see what you feel, see, sense or just know. If you do not get an answer, repeat the question and wait. If more than one individual is involved, go to the next person and follow the same process.

How To Eliminate Stress And Anxiety Through The Occult

Next, see rain falling on the flames. The flames get smaller and smaller. As they dwindle, so do your difficulties with the person or people. Watch as the flames dwindle until they are all out. The same as your difficulties with these people dissolve. Now, see a large, clear wall come up from the ground between you and the ones you had difficulty with. This wall protects you. You can hear others and deal with them from a safe distance.

You are protected.

Visualize yourself dealing with others and being safe, calm and relaxed. Know that these situations are minor, mundane, unimportant things in your life. You know that you are doing the best that you can and what you feel is right. Stay with that knowledge and relax.

Take a deep breath, smile and open your eyes.

Dealing With Separation Of Spouse Or Romantic Partner
Meditation:
(before starting refer back to the Beginning Meditation)

With your eyes closed, focus the color white or silver in front of you.

Visualize your lost partner in front of you. See the person as clearly as possible or just consciously be aware of how your partner looks.

Allow all the feeling you have to surface. Do not block any of it. Look at all your feelings. Positive and negative.

Take your time.

Visualize a giant clock which chimes in front of you. Listen to the repeating, cleansing sound. Become one with it. Immerse yourself in the sound. Blend with it.

With each sound of the chimes, allow yourself to feel lighter and more relaxed. With each chime, feel happier and more stable. The sounds cleanse your sadness and turn it into a brighter, lighter mood.

Your future becomes more and more light, happy and bright.

The sound of the chimes is uplifting and exhilarating. You feel yourself sitting with your spine straighter, your shoulders relaxed and a serene smile on your face.

You feel the chimes blend with your new mood. Lighter and lighter.

Let this feeling flow with you for a few moments. Take your time.

Know that anytime you hear the chimes, physically or in thought, you will automatically go into this wonderful mood.

Allow these new feelings to flow through you once again.

Relax. Take a deep breath and open your eyes.

How To Change How Others See You
Meditation:
(before starting refer back to the Beginning Meditation)

Breathe lightly and deeply to relax.

Visualize yourself and a loved one together. Begin to briefly look at the situation(s) that caused your division.

Allow yourself to rely on the strengths of the Earth, remembering that all relationships are built on solid foundations and stability. Envision the both of you seated in the midst of solid rock formations fashioned through time and various weather patterns – solar; wind; rain; snow. As these massive stones are standing, they are smooth, representing the ease of communication.

Know that these stones and caverns lend you protection from adverse conditions. They also represent loyalty. Stone is direct as it symbolizes being practical and down to earth. As you both begin to understand each other's uniqueness, like earthen stone, you see each has a special quality unto itself.

As you envision total agreement, you embrace, symbolizing an inseparable and indestructible relationship capable of long lasting association and partnership. The earthen stone can be both porous and solid depicting being open to new ideas, each other's directness and pure solidification of all ideas as purely one well-balanced idea.

Take a few breaths and feel yourself being well balanced in all ways.

When you feel ready, slowly open your eyes.

Reclaim Your Sexual Drive
Meditation:
(before starting refer back to the Beginning Meditation)

As you take a few slow breaths, see with your third eye a picture of a beautiful gleaming city. You stand on the outskirts and take in this environment. See skyscrapers and feel the activity, the motion and energy of the city.

Look up at the strong buildings reaching toward the sky.

Feel the energy moving to the center of the city.

You become aware that you have been standing outside too long. You are curious. You want to be part of the energy, which you feel is building up.

You walk to a street leading into the city. You step on the street and immediately feel a surge of joy, of fun and of energy flow throughout your body.

You feel uplifted and excited.

As you walk through the streets, you notice friendly, smiling people swiftly moving around you. You start to relax and enjoy the feeling. You feel as though you are part of this excitement and you have a feeling of coming home. You are safe and happy.

Look at the city and notice the colorful buildings and variety of stores and apartments. The people all happily bustling about.

How To Eliminate Stress And Anxiety Through The Occult

You realize you have been missing this feeling of excitement and being energetically alive.

You feel the pulse of the city moving at a comfortable, excited pace.

You know you are part of this. You move at the same speed and blend comfortably with your surroundings.

You are excited about all that you are capable of doing. You look forward to moving on your goals and achieving them.

Your life has become active, happy and full of movement and positive choices.

You feel the joy bubbling up inside of you.

You see a marching band coming down the street toward you and decide to join the march. You are enjoying yourself, becoming open and loving towards others. The people in the band are happy you joined them. They like you and welcome you as you march.

You feel loving energy toward everyone. As you send this energy and keep sending it in your daily life, you attract positive people to you.

Your heart is open to give and receive love. You keep this feeling from now on. It suits you. It is you. You are a vibrant, happy, loving person.

You are special and are meant to be filled with joy. You now allow all the good, loving, positive feelings to come into your being. You know that this is who you truly are.

Step away from the band and wave goodbye to them happily, for now.

You have made new friends and new opportunities for love.

As you walk through the city, keep yourself open to new relationships coming into your life.

You now attract these situations and have the excitement and energy to open up your life.

Stay relaxed and happy. Take your time in the city.

When you are ready, go back to the edge of the city.

Know that you are only leaving one city to go to your next place of safety, excitement and fun.

Breathe slowly a few times and open your eyes.

Rebuilding Self-Image
Meditation:
(before starting refer back to the Beginning Meditation)

Visualize a vibrantly colored garden. See all the plants and how pretty they are. Notice the green grass, and hiding in the bushes nearby, a few rabbits. They scamper about as you walk by and feel comfortable with you.

You see a grapevine and tall trees within a short distance.

You walk to where the luscious grapes are growing and sit on a large, flat wood stump next to them. You pick a few to eat and relax. Allowing all your tension to fall away as you enjoy the peace, quiet and the view.

You notice a shiny silver book nearby left on the grass.

You are curious, so you get up to pick the book up gently in your hands.

You notice, to your surprise, that in large, shiny silver letters your name is inscribed on the cover.

You walk back to your seat with the book. You are curious and happy that you found the book. In your heart, you know that it is important to you. It is a special gift meant only for you.

As you start to open the book in your hands, you immediately feel a surge of energy flowing through you.

How To Eliminate Stress And Anxiety Through The Occult

It makes you feel comfortable and excited at the same time.

You open the book to the first page. It reads – a list of all the things you should have accomplished by now.

You slowly turn the page and find that it is empty.

You turn the next page and it reads – you are EXACTLY where you should be. You are in your Right Place, Right Time, Right Situations. You are doing exactly what you should be doing at this time in your life. Everything you have done in the past was the right thing to do then.

You realize that you have done the best you can and are now ready to move on.

Turn the page once again. It is written - a list of all your accomplishments, abilities, all that you have done for others, your spiritual thoughts and your positive qualities.

As you turn the page, you notice pages and pages filled with positive writing all about you.

It is an endless list. As your life progresses, it will be added to.

You glance at the list and flip through the pages. You come to realize that you have many qualities you have not thought of. Qualities everyone else tells you that you have. You finally realize it is ok.

As you flip through the book, stop on and off to look at what is written. It could be a sentence, or just a word, such as – unique.

Take your time and look at as many as you wish.

Think it over. Think of different situations where those qualities came up.

Remember, you are a part of God and God creates wonderful unique things.

Take your time and let yourself feel good and happy about yourself. You are special and it is time you are aware of it.

Use this knowledge of yourself to consciously work with what you have. This is the time to add those qualities you wish to develop.

When you are ready, close the book. Stand up and place it on the tree stump you were sitting on. It is a safe place to leave it for now. You can always come back and look within the pages.

Walk to the garden and once again notice the colors and the scents. Enjoy yourself.

When you wish to, take a deep breath and open your eyes.

* Remember that you are unique with God's unlimited potential to be anyway you wish.

You are unique and have an abundance of positive qualities.

Erase Despair
Meditation:
(before starting refer back to the Beginning Meditation)

This is the time for you, with your eyes closed, to picture yourself on a hard wooden bridge. You feel the wooden railing and know it is safe and stable.

As you look up, you see the bridge ends at the beginning of a large courtyard. You walk to the end and step into the courtyard. The courtyard is surrounded by a tall, wooden, medieval-looking structure. It keeps everything negative outside.

You feel safe so that you can now take a deep breath and relax.

Look around you. You see colorfully-clothed people walking and smiling. On the right side of the yard, you see unending rows of military men at attention, some standing and some on horses. At the front of the line, in military garb, on horseback, you see the captain.

They seem to be waiting for something. You walk up to the captain and ask who is in charge.

The captain points to an iron door and tells you that the one in charge of all that you see is behind the door. You need only to open it.

You walk to the iron door and open it. To your surprise, you see a giant mirror and gaze upon yourself.

You realize that you are the one who controls everything in your life.

At any time you wish, you can call on your army to back you and be there for you. The army represents all your resources. All the abilities you normally do not think of, but are there, nonetheless.

Think back on all the times you have felt helpless or hopeless in your life.

You have always managed to call upon your military and come out of it.

Now is the time to call on them. Wake them from their inaction. Tell them what to do. Take action! You can overcome anything.

You have inner spiritual power and force. This gives you the ability to know that all things are possible.

You, as a Spiritual Force, cannot be denied. You have strength, energy and the power of the ages.

There is nothing that you cannot accomplish.

You see an altar next to you and placed on it are your shield, sword and your military clothing.

Go and put them on. As you do so, you begin to glow with White Light. You are invincible.

Call to the captain and army to let them know it is time to follow you and take action.

Look around you and with your troops start back toward the bridge. Wave goodbye to the people. They are there to show support.

Go on the bridge with your followers, knowing you can handle anything. Know that you have a bright, happy future ahead of you. This is only a short drawback that is ending NOW!

Feel your strength and happily move toward your bright future.

Take a deep breath, let it out slowly and open your eyes.

Attract Fun, Friendship And Love

Meditation:
(before starting refer back to the Beginning Meditation)

Be comfortable. Breathe slowly and deeply. Feel yourself inhaling and exhaling. Be aware of your mind and body being relaxed.

Let yourself visualize a spacious living room. Inside, you find comfortable surroundings with soft chairs, a large table with a lit candle in a candleholder. The flame is merely flickering and not large at all. You sit before the table and the candle in a comfortable chair.

You spread your hands so that your palms are facing the little flame, one hand on each side. Now, imagine that you are the Sun itself. It is your light that will make the flame grow. But first, you must place your heart and mind in the state of total love for all living things. As you do this, begin to visualize the Sun sending its loving rays into your mind. The rays then travel down your head, neck, shoulders, heart, arms and finally into your hands.

Your hands begin to develop miniature Suns in each palm. You can feel a miniature Sun growing within your entire being as well. You are NOW feeling the Loving Rays of the Sun as your own – As God's Light In You!

Now focus your total awareness onto the little flickering flame before you. Envision beams of light from your palms, heart and eyes.

Touch the base of the candleholder and the base of the candle. Watch the glowing, loving rays light up the entire candle. Think of this candle as your friend – A Loving Friend.

The cheerfulness begins to magnetize the flame. The flame bursts into a much larger, steadier flame – Filled with Gods Loving Light and Your Light of Love.

Hold the consciousness of the brightness of this new flame clear and steady. You feel your own joy rise and expand within you.

Your heart, like the candle's flame, is bursting into great joy and strength. Faith and confidence are renewed. And now the loving smile upon your face and within your heart is a living replica of the brilliant flame of Love reborn in you.

When you are ready, open your eyes,

You can do this meditation as many times as you like. Allow yourself to be open to newfound joy and love in your life.

How To Handle Unstable Kids And Disgruntled Workers
Meditation:
(before starting refer back to the Beginning Meditation)

Relax through deep breathing. Blend your consciousness with each atom of water. See each atom of water become a part of a greater whole.

Visualize the water moving and winding through the earth as a narrow stream of consciousness. See this and understand it represents a narrow relationship between you and a child or employee. There is a failing to allow openness toward each other.

As the water finds the winding way into a wider body of water, you can see this as your relationship and understanding of each other beginning to broaden. It is being affected by the surroundings – new ideas, new ways of growth and transformation.

See the water continue to flow out into an even larger and broader body of water, such as an ocean. The sense of openness promotes a wonderful healing with great flexibility and resilience. This is found in good relationships that become positive and communicative.

The rays of the Sun are gently reflected back into the sky. They comfortably burn away all blocks that get in the way of harmony and balance.

Listen with your heart, as well as your head, to what this person really means (not just what is being said).

As the water flows, so does your understanding open up to new horizons. You see past the limits and flow with the water to undiscovered understanding.

As you become more open and warm (from the Sun's rays), you notice the other person starts responding back in a more positive way.

This is like the water's waves, one flowing gently into another. It continues until there becomes a blending of the two waves.

Allow yourself to feel the flow of the water and the warmth of the Sun. Let yourself feel it and demonstrate it.

Be aware of how good it makes you feel.

Let yourself float with this feeling. Be serene, relaxed and happy. Nothing can disturb or upset you. You flow with the water's motion automatically and comfortably.

Be conscious of how you feel and, at a time that feels right to you, breathe deeply, smile and open your eyes.

MENTAL POWER AND FOCUS

Meditation:
(before starting refer back to the Beginning Meditation)

Deeply comfortable, keep your eyes closed. Breathe slowly.

Visualize an area where there are numerous trees and the earth, such as being in a park. These are ancient trees. You see a number of gnomes scurrying around. These are Earth-related gnomes and are here to give their support.

See yourself standing or sitting near the trees. Begin to adjust your breathing by inhaling and exhaling slowly and rhythmically. This rhythm calms down the body and mind. Soon your thoughts begin to slow down.

Now, you are ready to visualize your entire body as comfortably melting into the Earth. As it does, you begin to visualize cords of Light, growing out from your feet, like roots stretching and extending deep into the Earth itself. Going directly into her inner core.

These cords become extensions in which you release your anxieties and worries. To further help yourself, see these emotionally low energies being neutralized and transformed into more positive energy.

See them change from a darker shade of color to clear white or a yellowish white.

With your physical and emotional bodies being relaxed by the Earth, you are able to place greater focus on the surrounding trees.

Allow yourself to walk around any of the trees you see. Use your sensitivity by spreading your arms as you walk closer and closer. Pick a tree to have fun with and connect to. You are able to feel the tree's energy extended outward to embrace you.

Now, embrace it momentarily, giving yourself a few minutes to start feeling its soothing energy. What type of tree is it? Does it have green or colorful leaves? How thick is the trunk? What else do you notice?

As you tune into the tree's energy, you now start to place your consciousness deeply into the heart of the tree. The magnetism is building.

Now, the electrical flow is exchanged through your total embrace. Feel the spiritual energy of the tree flow deeply into your being and your heart.

Become aware of its ancient knowledge. The branches reach upward toward the celestial sky to gather information. The roots dig deeply into the Earth for stability, focus and grounding. The ancient trunk with its passage through time has an abundant storehouse of knowledge. It feels the weather, the animals and people who inhabit the surroundings, Earth information (such as Earthquakes). It is always growing and expanding, physically, as well as in knowledge.

Look at the stable, grounded tree. Feel it. You can ask questions later. Think of all you can learn from it. Study it from all angles. Take your time. Do not rush. It is a tree of wisdom and can answer any question. Take one question and ask it, then relax and wait for an answer. It can come as a color, feeling or some other form.

Relax and be comfortable.

You find it fun and exciting to be able to learn about any subject you can think of. The tree lets you know that you should look around you. It wants to point something out to you.

It is a beautiful day, with yellow flowers all around. You notice it makes you feel happy, interested and curious. You realize that at any time you choose to learn or to be stable and focused, this color helps you to keep on track. You know that in your physical life, you can surround yourself with this color or have anything yellow visually near you to keep you stable on your goal.

This knowledge makes you happy. Thank the tree for giving you this insight. Let go of the tree and take a few steps back.

You feel your connection to the tree.

Your legs become like the roots and your arms the branches. Your body becomes the trunk; your hands and the top of your head are the leaves.

Now you feel totally at peace and just like the tree – absorbing the rays of the Sun and the knowledge all around you. You feel stable and focused.

You absorb the rays, which pass through the leaves, as well as all knowledge that is now easily and effortlessly absorbed by you.

It is now fun and an exciting quest.

When you feel you are done, refocus on how your body normally looks, keeping these new feelings with you. You can always come back to this place.

Take a few breaths. You will awaken totally refreshed. Open your eyes.

Change Lack Of Satisfaction
Meditation:
(before starting refer back to the Beginning Meditation)

With your breath slowly and rhythmically moving through your body, be aware of your entire being relaxing.

Within a grove of trees, find a clearing that looks comfortable. There, build a blazing campfire.

Sit on the grass and look deeply into the flames.

As you do so, you become aware of some movement within the flame. You focus your attention on it and it becomes clearer.

You can see a salamander with a crown. You are seeing the essence of the Fire. The elemental "Spirit of the Fire."

He dances within the flames. Twisting, turning, growing and spinning. It is beautiful to watch.

You look on and feel your mood uplifted. You are relaxed, yet your energy is increasing quickly. You feel exhilarated.

As you watch, the salamander looks kindly at you. He asks why you feel dissatisfied.

You think about it before you speak. You take your time and tell him anything that may bother you. No matter how large or small.

As you talk about it, you look back to where each situation started.

Decide if it is something still affecting your life or not. Is it something you can change now?

Are there ways to control what caused these situations?

Once you have exhausted all your ideas and thoughts, relax.

The Salamander King now tells you that those situations no longer have an effect over you.

You feel warm, comfortable and at peace.

Now, he says to make a list of all the things that bring joy and satisfaction into your life. Such as: being able to drive a car; having fun with your friends; accomplishing a task you did well; etc.

Take your time and make the list as long as possible. Write your list on a scroll. When you are finished, look at your accomplishments with pride and joy.

Put the scroll in your pocket, so you can look at it and add to it whenever you choose.

Say goodbye to the elemental Spirit King. Watch him quickly disappear.

Next, let the fire burn out. Get up and walk back to the grove singing happily. Take a deep breath and open your eyes.

Counteract Unjust Treatment

Meditation:
(before starting refer back to the Beginning Meditation)

With your eyes closed, see yourself sitting on a cushioned wrought-iron bench in a park.

You see people quickly moving back and forth. Your energy is high, yet you are relaxed. You wonder where these smiling people are going. You are safe and among spiritual people.

You look around at all the warm colors of the flowers. You see crimson, pink, orange and purple.

As you relax among all this beauty, you feel lighter and more loving.

How To Eliminate Stress And Anxiety Through The Occult

Your loving feelings attract others who are positive to you. It is as though you have become a happy magnet.

You see people standing at a distance looking as though they would like to come nearer, but cannot. You recognize them. They are people who have insulted you or were unfair. Look at their faces. Notice how lonely and unhappy they are.

You know that they need to change themselves to become happy. You wish that you could help them join you and your happy exciting friends. You know that they are not ready to join the fun yet.

You send them love. Your loving Spiritual energy surrounds them in pink. You know they will eventually grow.

In the meantime, you realize they are like small children, petulant and interested in themselves. You are aware that you cannot take them seriously. Their attitudes do not hold any meaning for you.

You look at them once more and go back to your own happy, peaceful, fun and exciting life. You enjoy the people around you who are loving and positive, just as you are loving and positive to everyone.

Frolic in the park, sing and dance. Be happy. When you are ready, go back to your bench. Relax and enjoy the feeling of knowing you had a great day and that there are many more to come. Sit comfortably and open your eyes.

CHAPTER SIX

Benefits of Music

MUSIC is a universal language. Have you ever noticed that some music makes you sad, happy, energetic or changes your mood in some way?

Music can synchronize with the way you feel or it can be utilized to shift your awareness into a better positive mode.

Musicians utilize this tool to put you in a particular mood, energy level or emotional state.

Some healers will use music to alter your physical/emotional and psychological situation to improve them.

Music is connected to the elements and can be consciously utilized in numerous ways.

There are times when you will be more comfortable listening to one type of music more than another. Pay attention to this, as it will enable you to be consciously aware of what your elemental connection is. Then use that knowledge. As an example, if you feel best around drums at this time, you can increase sound and speed to give you more energy. You can also lower the pitch and slow the speed/rhythm down. This could put you in a more relaxed, open, meditative mind frame.

Some correlations between instruments and the elements are:

- <u>Earth</u> - is represented by drums and all percussion instruments
- <u>Air</u> - is represented by flutes and all wind instruments
- <u>Fire</u>- is represented by guitars and all string instruments
- <u>Water</u>- is represented by bells, cymbals and all resonant metals

Deep tones and slow sounds help to alter us from a hectic day. Major notes such as on the piano, C to B are connected to our chakras (energy centers). White keys are called natural tones. Notes are related to the chakras which are also connected to the same tones. The notes are as follows:

C – root chakra

D – sacral chakra

E – solar plexus chakra

F – heart chakra

G – throat chakra

A – brow chakra

B – crown chakra

For meditation, use A and B more, since those are connected to the head and are calming.

Music/sound, has been scientifically tested and shows that a form of metamorphose exists. They can test the brainwave change also, to see if the person tested is on a beta brainwave (as when we're speaking to someone) or on an alpha brainwave (meditation state).

How To Eliminate Stress And Anxiety Through The Occult

A visual way to test is the use of Kirlian photography. This is a camera that we build which shows a picture of your aura (energy field). Although it can also be used to do psychic readings, which I do, it can also help to show what emotional/physical/mental/spiritual state a person is in. These forms of pictures originated in Russia as a scientific experiment.

We have several tools available to us to show the impact of music. However, you need to be aware that these influences have been with us for centuries.

When you think of such sounds as mantras (which use sound vibration), bells in temples, gongs, hymnals and drumming, they all share a common ground. Rhythm and music can shift you into a calm, meditative state.

The relaxation this can give you, even without a specific situation to convert, can be invaluable.

Think of the times you listened to some of the classical, romantic or slower music. Do you remember how you felt? Your physical body automatically relaxes, as well as your stress level.

Use music consciously to control situations and help you to achieve your goals.

Try it. Play with it and have fun.

How To Eliminate Stress And Anxiety Through The Occult

CHAPTER SEVEN

Environmental Meditation

HOW and when you meditate are very important factors.

Your environment has a very direct impact on you. It can enhance your meditative experience or detract from it.

It would be more difficult to become relaxed in a chaotic environment. That does not mean that it is not possible. Simply that it is not as conducive to meditation.

It is best to be in a calm, quiet and comfortable place. Adjust your clothing so that there isn't any tightness around the neck, wrist, waist and ankles.

Remember that meditation is the gateway to true knowledge and the power to gain your goals.

In guided meditation, you focus on what you are manifesting and at the same time you are letting go and allowing your goal to come into the physical reality.

Where you set your mental awareness consistently is what you bring into or cancel in your life.

You will notice how this also generates synchronicities. Basically, meaningful coincidences. As an example, when you decide you want to buy a certain type of car, like a convertible, all of a sudden you see them everywhere.

When you add choosing the correct environment

to your meditation, it will be easier. It will also put you into the meditative state faster.

Your environment is represented by your surroundings, the people around you and other situations. In this chapter, our focus is on your physical surroundings, such as mountains, water, sun, warm areas, etc.

Some environments are also connected to the elements. When you meditate in conjunction with the elements, you are placing yourself into the stream of energy that best works for your intent.

Elements are the four creative energies of the Universe-Earth, Air, Fire and Water. They work together in harmony. Each element has numerous connections. We as spiritual beings can use this knowledge to enhance our meditative experiences. Some of these connections are as follows:

> <u>Earth</u> – Forest, cave, mine, canyon, mountain, grove, garden, orchard, hill, valley, park, farm, field, boulder, rock, beach, all forms of wood, clay, gem, stone and earth.
>
> <u>Air</u> – Places that have movement of air, like a mountaintop, the plains (wind), airport, sky, towers, travel agency, study/learning environments like a library, any movement connected to air.
>
> <u>Fire</u> – Flames, kitchen (oven/heat), volcano, lava, fireplace, campfire, smokestack, places with heat or fire, also energetic places.
>
> <u>Water</u> – Rain, ocean, stream, spring, lake,

fountain, shower, bathtub/water, fog, pool, well, steam room, geyser, sea shell, all water related places.

Knowing some of these connections helps you to either physically meditate in the listed places or to use them to create places/situations. In your meditations, you can use one element or combine them. As an example you can create a guided meditation yourself.

First pick your intent. Do your protection first.

Now, see yourself on a path (you choose the type – dirt, paved, etc.) and you walk on this path to the base of a tall mountain.

As you walk, look around at your surroundings. Where do you choose to be? What colors, sounds, textures or tastes are along your path? Take your time. Relax. You are not in a rush.

Now, look up at the mountain and be aware of how it looks. What is on it? Are there others or animals? How many? How close or far from you? Does the path continue? Is it a new one? Or does the mountain not have a definite path to follow?

Look around. Are there birds? Is it day or night? What is the weather? Are you warm or comfortable?

Check to see what your mood is. Is it happy, relaxed, anxious, curious or another feeling?

Look down at yourself and see what you are wearing. Is it in color?

Now, as you proceed up the mountainside, look at

the top. Know that you can reach it easily and effortlessly. Choose when you will get there. Take your time. Look again along the way.

As you reach the top, you feel the soft touch of the wind on your face. It feels good. Look at the mountaintop and start walking ahead toward a stream. When you get there, sit on a flat rock next to it. Relax for a short time. Get up and build a campfire next to the stream.

Now, as you watch the flames, focus on your goal. Picture it happening in the flame. See it, or know that as you think it, you create it.

When you feel you are done, get up and look at the flames. You will leave them to burn out in their own time.

Turn around to the direction you came from and retrace your steps.

In a relaxed, happy state, start to go down the mountain.

You feel happy, since you know that what you picked as your intent is now becoming reality.

As you come to the base of the mountain, look around, then go forward on the path you originally started on.

When you feel you are back at the beginning of the path, take a deep breath and open your eyes.

As you can see, this meditation utilized all the

elements. Earth (path, mountain, rock), Air (wind on your face), Fire (campfire, flame) and Water (stream).

Take your time to create your own. Write your meditation down first, so you know exactly what you want prior to starting. You will either remember it or use a cassette tape to record it so you can play it at your convenience.

Remember that you can go back to the same place as often as you like.

To give you an idea of how this works, I have included a sample for you.

Do your protection first and get yourself into the mediation state.

If you choose to meditate in your home or place of business, remember that utilizing the environmental connections is optional.

Manifesting Quick Money

Visualize yourself sitting in the chair that you are in now.

Notice how relaxed and calm you are feeling. Feel the warmth of the room and know you are safe and comfortable.

Take three deep breaths slowly. As you breathe in, think of money with wings coming to you quickly. As you breathe out, think of all negative energy leaving you.

Now visualize yourself getting up from the chair with a smile and a happy mood. See yourself picking up your mail. There are many envelopes, all bulging. They look like they will burst open.

As you open one, a lot of money falls out and into your hands. You keep opening envelopes and each one is stuffed with money. Envelopes are all over the place. It seems that the more you open, the more the envelopes multiply. After a while, you open your last envelope. This envelope has a yellow piece of paper with writing on it. You read it. It says – Anytime you choose, you can come back for the mail and there will be more envelopes bursting with money.

You put the money in a safe place with the note.

Now, you know that any time you choose, money will come to you for your goals. Go back to your seat. Relax. Take one more deep breath and slowly open your eyes.

If you choose to meditate in your home or place of business, remember that utilizing the environmental connection is optional.

CHAPTER EIGHT

Tools For Meditation

THERE are an unlimited number and variation of tools to be utilized for meditation purposes to cancel stress.

I am giving you a few examples that work. At different times in our lives, we are attracted to different methods. This is because our subconscious mind and spiritual being know which will work best for us in each situation or time. You will have a "pull" or interest in the method that is correct for you. Pay attention to it, then take action and move on it.

Trust in Divine Power and yourself to bring you safely to your destination and in a positive form.

Remember to always do protection, then get into your meditation state. If you are using a physical tool (stones, etc.) place them in your lap or loosely in your hand placed on your lap.

MEDITATION AND PRAYER

When these two forms of power are combined, they are unstoppable.

They release the force of spiritual power to handle and overcome your obstacles.

<u>You</u> have the ability to change your world.

Rely on Divine Power to make your Path stress

How To Eliminate Stress And Anxiety Through The Occult

free and secure.

Release your stress and let God handle your situation. Allow yourself to feel positive. Know that as you ask, you are already being answered. In the Bible, in Matthew 7:7 & 7.8 it says – "Ask, and you will receive; seek, and you will find; knock, and the door will be opened to you. For everyone who asks will receive and anyone who seeks will find, and the door will be opened to him who knocks." Which metaphysically means: <u>Ask</u>- in prayer <u>Seek</u> –looking to do positive/to please God, <u>Knock</u> – go out and look.

You can substitute your own terminology for God, depending on your Belief System.

You do not need to stay in a state of stress. You can achieve calm, serenity and inner peace.

When conflicting thoughts, chaos, disillusion or negativity enter your life, remember that Divine Power is your Source of Peace. Call on God through prayer in meditation. Trust in God. Let go and let God take over. Remember Matthew 17:20 – "For truly I tell you, if you have faith the size of a mustard seed, you will say to the mountain, 'Move from here to there,' and it will move; and nothing will be impossible for you."

How To:

After you do your protection, get into your meditative state.

Once you are relaxed, with your eyes closed, visualize a white or golden white screen across from your third eye (middle of forehead).

Say your prayer mentally or verbally. Stay aware of any pictures you might "see" on your screen so you remember them for later.

Also be aware if you see colors, hear sounds or all of a sudden get an idea. These are all forms of answers to you, connected to what stressful situation you pray to change.

You may use any of the following prayers I wrote for you or create your own to de-stress. The prayers in meditation do not need to be long. They must be sincere and prayed with focus and a feeling of expectancy. After all, you know that you will be answered.

Now give it a few minutes after the meditative prayer and pay attention to any input. You may receive it right away or within three days, such as all of a sudden coming up with an idea, feeling or urge. Pay attention to it. Move on it. Trust it. After all, look at where your answer came from.

When you are finished, say thank you before you open your eyes. Giving thanks is a very important part of the process.

Prayer One – say or think – I know that with God, all things are possible. Where I am, there also is God. Through God, I now turn my situation around and cancel stress. The situation I now change is (<u>fill in your</u>

goal).

Prayer Two – say or think – Divine Power flows through me and around me. God and I are One. We are always connected. God, Grant me a way out of my stressful situation. Change negative to positive. Guide me in how to correctly transform my situation to achieve inner peace. Thank you for helping me to transform (fill in situation). Then "see" the situation being replaced by a positive one.

Prayer Three – say or think – I know that Divine Power is with me. God wants me to be happy, successful, calm, the way I was meant to be. Divine Power and I now change my situation from (fill in situation) to (fill in what your intent is). I work with Divine Power to make this happen. Thank you Divine Power. So Be It.

Prayer Four – say or think – I acknowledge God as my Source. He brings inner peace, tranquility and joy into my life. I now cancel stress (fill in situation) and manifest (fill in new, positive situation). Thank you, God.

Prayer Five – say or think – God shows me the way. I listen, love and speak to others in the way I want them to treat me. I respect others and find positive qualities in them. I thus attain calm, peace and harmony. What I do, and put out to others, comes back to me one hundred fold.

Thank you, God. So Be It.

Prayer Six – say or think – I fully trust in Divine

Power to clear the way to peace, harmony and relaxation with enthusiasm. My transformation is at hand. I advance in the knowledge that all is well. I change (fill in situation) to (fill in goal). I create my world. Thank you, Divine Power. It Is So.

Prayer Seven – say or think – I achieve peace, calm and balance in my life. I Let Go and Let God. I listen to the voice of God within me. This is my turning point. I transform (fill in situation) to a positive (fill in goal). I now give it to God to take care of for me. Thank you, God. So Be It.

DE-STRESS WITH GEMSTONE MEDITATION

Gemstones have a frequency/vibration of their own. They can connect to ours to heighten abilities, increase awareness, attract positive situations, cancel negative ones, take away stress and depression as well as other things.

The science community has been able to take photos of the energy field surrounding minerals, rocks, stones and gemstones to prove the energy exists.

The size of the stone does not matter for our purpose. Nor does it matter if it is a raw stone or polished.

What does matter is that it should not have any negative vibrations attached to it from an outside source, such as an upset sales person holding it, or the stone being owned previously by a negative person. We need to cancel any negative energy that might reside in the stone prior to utilizing it. Sometimes, from frequently wearing a stone in negative situations, it can be drained of energy. It needs to be charged back to its normal level so that the only energy emanating from it is its own balance state.

You can do this a few ways. Five of these methods are:

#1 – Put the stone in indirect or direct sunlight for a minimum of three days. As an example, on your window sill.

#2 – Use a bowl, cup or whatever is convenient for you. Bury the whole stone in sea salt (found in your supermarket) for a minimum of three days in the container. Then you can utilize it.

#3 – Hold it under running water for at least three to five minutes, such as a river, stream or kitchen faucet.

#4 – You can put it into the freezer for a minimum of three days.

#5 – You can also place it on a flat piece of Selenite stone very effectively, for a three day minimum.

When your stone is "clear", you can utilize it for meditation.

How To:

Hold the gemstone in your hand. Whichever hand feels comfortable to hold it with at the time.

Choose a guided meditation to work with. Then sit in your chair. Lay the stone on your lap or hold it in your hand (placed on your lap so it doesn't fall).

Proceed with the guided meditation technique.

The following gemstones are good for these guided meditations to cancel stress in various situations:

Stone	Meditation Purpose
Blue Calcite	Removes emotional blocks
Red Calcite	Drains away negative emotions
Spider Web Jasper	Valium type effect, soothing feeling
Lepidolite	Enables you to feel at peace
Imperial Topaz	Makes you feel you have enough mental abilities to handle situations
Fire Opal	Helps you to take action in a situation where it's needed
Blue Tiger Eye	Gives your body energy and enhances your productivity
Black Jade	Helps you to balance and deal with power, sex and survival situations. Gives you inner strength.

Some of the stones contained in my book "Psychic Vibrations of Crystals, Gems and Stones" can also be utilized for this type of meditation. Such as:

STONE	MEDITATION PURPOSE
Lapis Lazuli	Improves self-assurance, increases psychic/intuitive attunement, strengthens the body
Opal	Stops anger
Topaz	Takes away night fears
Peridot	Takes away fear, guilt, depression
Tourmaline	Helps to release negativity
Bloodstone	Gives you courage
Crazy Lace	Creates harmony, peace
Beryl	Overcomes lazy attitudes
Carnelian	Enhances courage, calms the nerves

MEDITATION WITH HERBAL APPLICATIONS

Herbs have frequencies that we can tune into to alleviate stressful situations. These frequencies mesh with our own to create peace, harmony, balance, as well as numerous other situations.

Do your protection prayer, sit comfortably, place the herb on your lap or place your hand on your lap holding the herb loosely. Proceed with your meditation.

I am listing some of the herbs which are conducive for canceling stress in different conditions. These herbs help during meditation so you can quickly achieve your goals. Remember to match the herb with your meditation intent.

Herbs	Meditation Purpose
Basil	Harmony
Lilac	Harmony, gives you ideas in meditation on how to cancel
Vanilla	Heighten low energy
Cedar	Heightens your courage so you can easily overcome situations
Gardenia	Harmony, peace
Nutmeg	Situations with fidelity, money, business luck
Vervain	Calm, helps move you into meditative state easier
Sweetpea	Attract friendship, increase strength, courage
Jasmine	Helps you to meditate, calm
Caraway	For general negativity to be cancelled
Hyacinth	Peace and helps you to meditate
Passion Flower	To calm problems, situations dealing with friendship
Cumin	Brings peace
Acacia	Helps you to meditate
Magnolia	Peace, situations dealing with fidelity

Rose	Calm, peace, harmony, tones down arguments
Ivy	Fidelity, luck, general negativity
Quince	Accidents, general negativity
Olive	Peace, lust, fertility, luck
Myrtle	Peace, fidelity, money, love
Morning Glory	Harmony, happiness

Ancient Oil Meditation

Oils have been utilized for centuries to aid in meditation. Ancient civilizations understood their powers and put them to use. In meditation, as well as for other purposes, numerous oils were considered sacred. They were looked at as a link between mankind and nature.

Natural oils made up one of the earliest trade items in ancient times.

For our purpose, we combine oils with the state of meditation.

When you have said your protection prayer, put a few drops of the oil in the palms of your hands and a drop under your nose. Then sit in a comfortable chair and proceed with your meditation techniques.

Make sure you match the oil with your intent.

The essential oils are the best. Do not blend the oils. Do not get an oil that has other scents added.

Oil	Meditation Purpose
Rose	Calm, harmony, peace serenity, tones down arguments, lust
Iris	Love, intuition improvement
Lime	Physical energizing, use with visualization for protection
Cinnamon	Intuition, prosperity, success
Honeysuckle	Weight loss, psychic awareness, prosperity
Orange	Joy, energizing
Apple	Happiness, love, peace

Incense Meditation

Incense is very versatile and utilized by numerous cultures. Incense, for various reasons, has been around since the ancient world.

The scent helps to put you in a state of mind that when used in conjunction with meditation can give you very beneficial results.

All incense, when burned, clears your meditation area of negativity. You can use it to help you meditate in a safer environment (except for Myrrh - by itself, <u>not</u> to be used).

The incense is not meant to be used as a focus,

just to "clear" your area and help put you into a mindset that increases your meditative abilities. The fragrance automatically works. Choose the incense that matches with the vibrations of your goal.

Incense is made from diversified sources. Fruits, leaves, flowers, oils, to name a few. The scent helps you to be in the right state of consciousness, so you can meditate on your goal. They come in a variety of forms, such as: Stick, cone, powder, block and incense papers.

Remember to say your protection prayer, light the incense, then sit in your chair and continue your meditation technique.

Incense	Meditation Purpose
Pine	Money, fertility, healing, protection
Magnolia	Fidelity
Patchouli	Fertility, love
Lavender	Happiness, peace
Hydrangea	Cancel negativity
Lily of the Valley	Mental ability, happiness
Marigold	Legalities
Apple	Love, happiness, peace
Hyacinth	Love, peace

Orange	Luck, energizing
Orchid	Love
Bodhi (also called Bo-tree)	Meditation
Rose	Spiritual insight
Musk	Lust

<u>Candles And Guided Meditation</u>

Candles are not meant to be used as a meditation focus. They are for concentration, which helps you to move into meditation. Remember to say your protection prayer first. Light a white, yellow or purple candle as you sit in your chair.

Gaze at the candle flame until you can see all the colors in it and around it. Look at the white, the blue, the red in it. Watch its movements, back and forth, up and down, and in different directions.

When you feel that you have a strong awareness of how it looks, close your eyes. Relax.

Now visualize the flame in your mind at the third eye level (in the middle of your forehead) and a little in front of you. Recreate the flame, feel it, sense it, be detailed. Hold this image in your mind as long as you can. Then relax.

Then let the image go and go into your meditation

technique. This visualization helps you to focus and become centered so that you may have a better meditation.

When you can see the flame clearly as you visualize, you will also have developed the ability to visualize your goals clearly when you are in your meditative state.

One of my meditation students used the candle method to help her to learn how to focus and visualize a particular goal.

Previously, she always had trouble with both focus and visualization.

At the time, she was working on studying for a degree in nursing. She wasn't able to keep her focus during study times.

Use of the candle in her meditation helped her to develop her focus. Also, she learned how to better visualize her goal to create and excel in her studies. She is now enjoying a rewarding career as a professional nurse.

How To Eliminate Stress And Anxiety Through The Occult

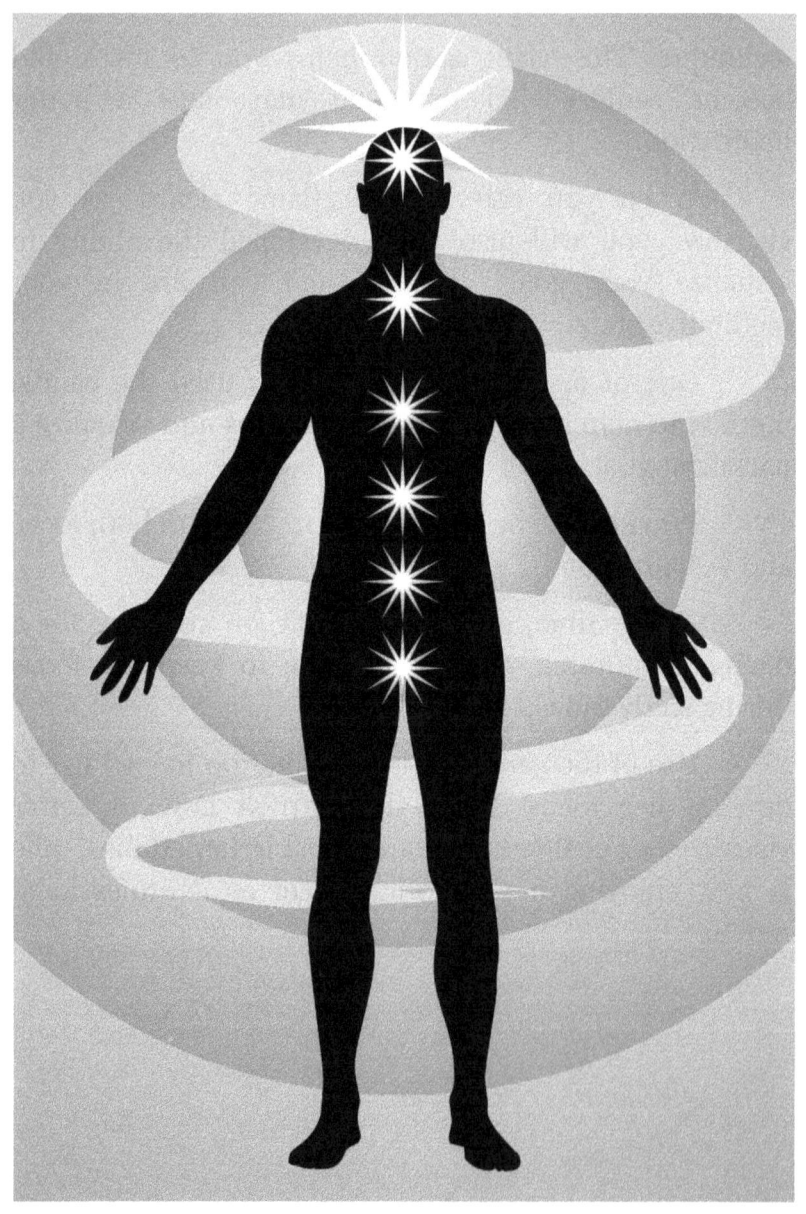

CHAPTER NINE
Magickal Formulae

THROUGH time, formulae have come down through the Mystery Schools such as mine: "The D'Andrea School of Esoteric Studies." These formulae have worked for centuries, thus we know they create specific situations.

Magickal intentions, focus and expectancy are your tools for empowerment. Use these spells to create a better, happier life – now.

1- Peace Of Mind Spell

To create peace of mind in your life, do the following:

Tools:

Blue ink or carving tool

1 yellow candle – any size

A little of the herb called cumin

Angel connection – Vohn Manah

Start on a Sunday.

Take a yellow candle and write in blue ink or carve (use a knife or anything that leaves an imprint) your first name on it at the top around the wick.

Sprinkle a little cumin on top of the candle and put some near the candle to carry with you later.

You can sprinkle some in your wallet or whatever you carry within three feet of your body.

Focus on your mind becoming quiet and peaceful.

Light the candle and as you do so, focus on saying the following:

"I am now protected by Divine Power."

Then:

"Through the Power of Fire and Flame,

I now invoke thee to obtain,

Peace of mind I now ordain,

Through Power of the Eternal Flame.

"I call on angel Vohn Manah,

To bring good thoughts,

And to inspire.

So Be It."

Now let the candle burn to the bottom and then throw the remainder outside of your home. When this is completed, carry the herb with you in your pocket, wallet, pocketbook or anywhere that is within a three-foot range of your body.

2- Peace Of Mind Spell

My message to you is that you can't worry. You did not want to attract/create that situation in your life. Everything will be all right through Divine Power.

Relax, let go of worry, frustration, limitations. Do the following spell with an open heart, breathe slowly and let Divine Power's White Light flow through you and surround you.

Feel the Blessings of the Universe come to you.

Tools:

Violet or purple cloth or pouch

Violet flowers

Bowl or cup of water

Take a piece of violet or purple cloth or pouch that you have not utilized before and lay it down on a flat surface as an altar or base cloth.

On top of this, place a bowl or cup of water.

Place fresh or dried violet flowers around the bowl or cup to make a circle.

Place the flowers clockwise to create peace, calm a temper and get rid of anxiety.

Place a few flowers into the water. Take three slow, deep breaths. Hold your hands, palms down, over the water. Focus on becoming calm and keep breathing slowly.

Say the following:

"I am Protected by the Divine and the Divine In Me"

Next say:

"I now release the Flowers' Power,

Calm and steady comes its shower,

Of the Light we know is Guided,

By the hand of Angels forces.

"I call on Venus,

Calm and loving,

Come to me and help me grounding.

Thank you, Divine Power.

Thank you, Isis.

So Be It."

Then take the water with the flowers and place in a bucket. Use this water to mop floors or sprinkle around your home. Take some of the ones around the cup and place some under your bed and carry some with you. When under stress, think of where these flowers are.

3- Peace Of Mind Spell

During the time of the New Moon, it is a good time to create what you want in your life including: peace, de-stressing and inner calm.

This is the time to release stress and situations holding you back or blocking you from your rightful life of peace and happiness.

Engrave the following on a piece of wood or paint with blue ink:

> *"Isten mindig vigyaz ram,*
>
> *Minden mindig jo."*

Then sit quietly holding it and breathe slow and deep as you think of a scene that relaxes you. Such as: a vacation you loved in the past or a goal you have that's happy and see it achieved.

Think of a blue light above you, coming down and surrounding you and through you.

Focus this light into your wood talisman.

Next, carry this with you each time you get upset, stressed or anxious and touch it or hold it in your hand.

4-Peace Of Mind Spell

The Power of the Word is ancient, old Power. Utilized through time and space. Through this dimension to gates/portals to extra-dimensions. It is totally non-limited by any form of energy.

The Word has no limitations. The magick is hidden in it.

If used mentally, it works. If used verbally, it has more Power behind it due to vibrational forces. I suggest the Spoken word whenever possible.

The Bible, other religious material and occult written sources have hidden Power Words contained in them.

Tools:

Bible

White candle

Frankincense

Do the following:

First, breathe slowly for a minute. Then light the Frankincense.

Next, light the white candle. Sit or stand facing them quietly and keep your breath slow and smooth.

Focus on your heart opening and releasing all negativity accrued from others. Focus on inner calm, peace and your heart

Open the Bible and pray Psalm 39, Verse 12 whenever you need it:

"Hear my Prayer, O Lord, and give ear unto my cry; hold not thy peace at my tears; for I am a stranger with thee, and a sojourner, as all my fathers were."

Read this verbally seven times with reverence and conviction from your heart.

Know in your heart that this is so.

5-Peace Of Mind Spell

Take the Tarot card called The Sun or get a picture of the sun. Photocopy it. Put this copy into direct sunlight for 3 days.

Next, hold it in your hand and focus on what you want:

To become calm, less stressed and successful in your endeavors.

Place this copy in a yellow pouch, medicine bag or mojo bag. Carry it and allow it to magnetically work for you.

6-Peace Of Mind Spell

The Shamanic Way is to manifest through Power, intent and knowledge. All life is a circle. All life is cyclical.

Remember Karma – what you do comes back to you. Or- As you sow, so shall you reap. Thus, the circle. So remember to always do only positive.

Stand in a place you will not be disturbed.

With white chalk, draw a circle around you, going clockwise. Do not have any breaks in the line as you draw the circle. If you do, start again.

Focus on the Great Spirit of Mother Earth and Father Sky protecting you and holding your energy in safety and peace. Now, making you invincible, relaxed and safe.

Know that all around you is their energy.

Chant the following words, rhythmically:

"Mother earth, Father Sky, Come to me and be my Guide."

Do this seven times, then wait a minute, repeat five times, wait a minute, then repeat seven times again.

Stay centered until you feel the urge that you are finished. Then in a counter-clockwise direction, scatter and rub out the circle.

Walk away, knowing you are taken care of.

 # 7 – Peace Of Mind Spell

The herb called Vervain was utilized in ancient times. This herb is connected to the Deities known as: Thor, Jupiter, Isis, Venus, and Kerridwen, among others.

This herb connects to the element of Earth.

Earth energy can be grounding to calm and de-stress you.

Tools:

Vervain

Water

Rose Incense

Take some Vervain, boil water in a pot (ratio-about 1 Tablespoon herb: 1 cup water) and add the herb. Boil for 15–20 minutes. Strain and keep the herb.

This infusion can now be used to add to your bucket of water. Use this, without anything else added to the water, to mop your floors. If you have a rug, simply sprinkle some on it. Do this in every room to bring peace and calm.

Next, burn Rose Incense in the rooms for the scent and for these vibrations to replace the negative energy the room might be holding, especially from arguments, with harmony, peace and love.

For centuries Shamans, Druids and other disciplines have utilized this herb.

At the time of sunrise, say:

"I am now under the Protection of <u>(pick one of the above Deities)</u> (Ex: Isis) through Divine Power."

Hold the herb in your hand and put your intent on your heart, bring through visualizing the energy of the herb around you and surrounding you. Feel or think of this energy bathing you in its calm, protective energy.

When you are done, place this herb next to your bed.

8 – Peace Of Mind Spell

We are emerging from the Third Dimension and moving up toward the Fifth. Fourth Dimensional Reality is basically new, starting with energy from the heart chakra. The Fifth means you can instantly manifest.

So as you think, you are a magnet for attracting that thought. Being this is so, stress can be completely eliminated.

Put your intent on being calm, relaxed, self-confident and joyous.

Blend the following and place in a blue pouch or material. When done, tie it closed with three knots and focus on your intent while mixing them.

Tools:

Place in a blue pouch/medicine bag:

Peridot-one stone

Pink lavender-herb

Three drops of Peace Oil or Jojoba Oil

Tie closed. Put a drop of the oil on your neck and shoulders. This helps you to move ahead in your life happily.

Then carry the pouch with you.

9 – Peace Of Mind Spell

The positive properties from candles add action and energy for creating a stress free environment.

Tools:

Blue candle - any size

Vervain – herb

Frankincense - incense

Sodalite – the blue stone

Cup or bowl

Do this spell on a Sunday.

Use a blue candle and light the Frankincense while focusing your intent on peace.

Place the stone called sodalite next to the candle. Add it to a cup or bowl with the herb vervain.

Say the following with sincerity and focus:

"Upon this earth,

I call in Peace,

Throughout this time,

I walk in Peace.

"From sun to moon,

From moon to sun,

I dwell in love,

Within my heart."

Leave everything where they are until the candle burns to the bottom.

Next, place the herb near your bed. (Within three feet of your body.) Take the stone and carry it with you at all times.

Take the candle and incense remains and bury them in the ground.

Know in your heart that this is done.

10 – Peace Of Mind Spell

To bring peace to your home or office, the following spell will attract this energy from the Ethers.

First say:

"I am now Protected by Divine Power,

I am now surrounded by Divine Power,

I am now infused by Divine Power,

And let there be Peace, Peace, Peace.

And So It Is."

Next, say the following incantation to invoke these Guardians:

"By the Dragons of Earth,

By the Dragons of Sky,

By the Dragons of Fire,

By the Dragons of Water.

"I now invoke pure peace of mind,

My home is safe,

My home is free,

Only positive energies,

Come with me.

And As I Say, So Shall It Be."

Every time there is an argument or discord in your home, light a Rose Incense in the room in which the discord took place so the vibration of the home is reset to peace, harmony and balance. You can also do this in an office or other surroundings. (In these cases, you may put the flower called the rose in the room, but it must have the scent.)

You can also carry rose petals in a sachet, bag or add it to your bath water.

 # 11 – Peace Of Mind Spell

Magickal Oils work vibrationally and through scent. At times, color is also a factor. Scents have been utilized as a trigger from ancient times. The brain reacts to these vibrations automatically.

Any of these oils can be utilized by putting a drop or two on your body. Place the drops on your heart, throat or neck.

Oils can be added to medicine bags, mojo bags, pouches, sachets, poppets, baths, poultice, incense, soaps, floor washes, talisman, amulets, clothing, hair rinse, among other forms.

Focus your intent on only the positive.

Oils for peace, harmony, de-stressing and joy:

Cherry – connected to Venus

Fir – connected to Jupiter

Lavender – connected to Mercury

Rose – connected to Venus

Wood – connected to Earth

12 – Peace Of Mnd Spell

To remove a hex, a jinx or any crossed condition to gain peace, do the following:

Tools:

Gray candle

Bergamot Oil

Rosemary Oil

Bible

Sea salt

1 – On a Wednesday, anoint a Gray Candle with Bergamot Oil and Rosemary Oil.

2 – Read all of Psalm Seven - four times, with focus, as you burn the candle to the socket.

3 – Also, sprinkle some Bergamot Oil and some Sea Salt throughout your home, especially in all doorways leading out of your home. Rub your hands lightly with some Sea Salt also.

When you are finished with the candle, throw it away outside your home.

13 – Peace Of Mind Spells

Create the peaceful home that you deserve.

Tools:

Light blue Seven Day candle

Peaceful Home Oil or Success Oil

Parchment paper

Pen with black ink

High John Incense

Helping Hand Incense

Begin on the day of the new moon. Anoint a Light Blue Seven Day Candle with Peaceful Home Oil or Success Oil.

Write the word "Peace" nine times on a square of parchment. Do this with black ink. Set it beneath the candle.

Light some High John Incense and then the candle. Concentrate for about a half hour on harmony, love and understanding being in the home, rather than friction, confusion and disappointment. Extinguish the candle after this half hour by covering it with something – like aluminum foil. Do not blow it out with your breath.

The next day, burn Helping Hand Incense as you meditate over the candle flame. Alternate the two incenses each day until you have brought and restored peace and good will back to the home.

14 – Peace Of Mind Spell

Protection of your home is a priority. Without a safe home, how can you have peace?

Mix together the following ingredients: Rosemary, Basil, Dill Seeds, St. John's Wort and Sea Salt.

Sprinkle a little in each room of your home.

Sprinkle some Violet Oil in each room a well. As you sprinkle the oil and blend, intone:

"Guardian wolves across the land,

Protect my home from all that's bad,

From physical to astral plane,

Through dark of night and brightest day.

So Be It!"

Take a bath in Seven Holy Herbs Bath.

Read Psalm 118 seven times.

Anoint your body with Violet Oil after you dry off.

How To Eliminate Stress And Anxiety Through The Occult

CHAPTER TEN
Mandalas, The Mystical Circle

A mandala is a Sanskrit word (India), loosely meaning circle or mystical circle. It is considered one of the Forms-With-Power. It represents wholeness and unity plus change. After all, when you look at nature, it consists of myriads of circles and is cyclical. They do say life is a circle for good reason.

Take a good look at nature. The center of a flower, a whirlwind, tornado, magick circles, ancient sites, the planets and the Earth itself. Look around you and you will see circle upon circle in all different things. Just look with Sacred Geometry.

With a shamanic outlook you will notice that the dances are in a circle as they connect to the sky and earth and the base of a tipi is also a circle. The dream catcher is circular and the weave is toward the center, so it can be utilized as a mandala. The Medicine Wheel is used by the Europeans and the Native Americans. It is a Sacred Wheel, like the mandala. The intention is

How To Eliminate Stress And Anxiety Through The Occult

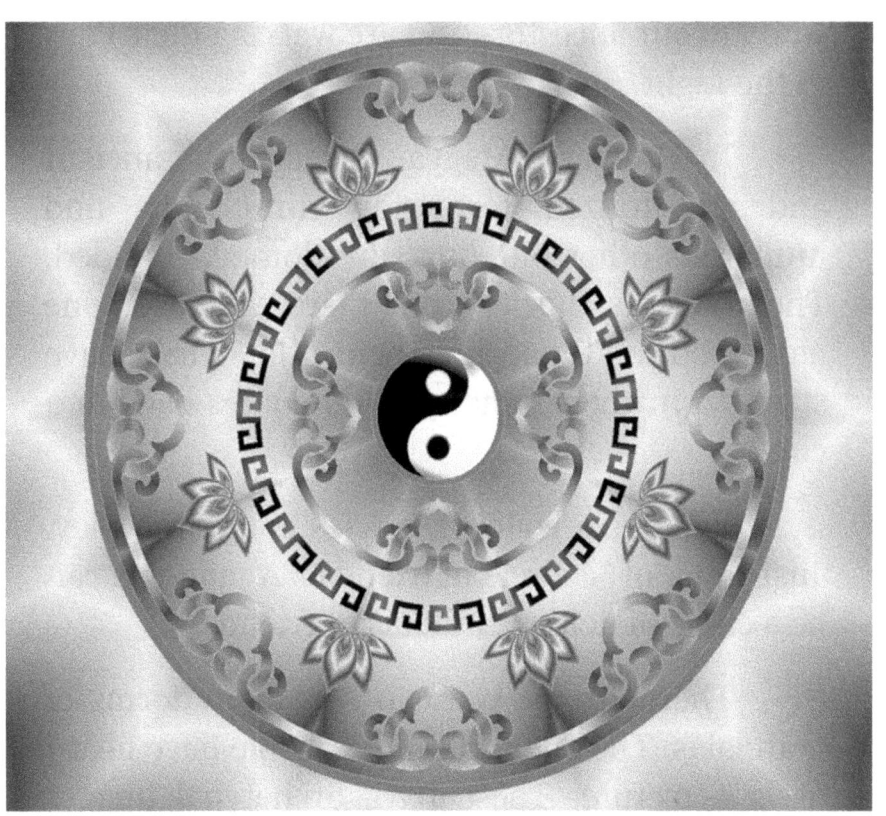

to offer prayer and rites which honor those who walk the Sacred Path on Earth, as well as those who are our ancestors and are walking their Path in the Light.

In Hungary (Magyar Orszag), the ancient and still-utilized form for yurts, huts and numerous other buildings are domed, rounded. The concepts this expresses are that everyone has good and bad in them, the weak have strength in them, what you do comes back in a circle.

Even as a concept, circles come into play. Just think of "a circle of friends." A mandala can be a circle of deities, animals or friends.

There are, as you can see, many forms of mandalas. The one form most people have heard of is a picture. These have archetypal images that come from deep within the mind. This is an expression of the Soul Mind at a deep level. The pictures are sometimes black and white, sometimes in color. They draw you in. Some are very elaborate, some are simple, but they all have that "pull." When you look at these pictures, you will find different ones resonate to

How To Eliminate Stress And Anxiety Through The Occult

your energies at different times. You may feel attracted to one that is very "busy" or one that just has a few lines. You may be "pulled" toward one that has a lot of color or black and white. You may also be attracted to various colors. You should always pick out your own mandala because what resonates for you at that time may not be the one someone else picks for you. They are going by what resonates to their energy.

Mandalas represent a time when color, sound, light, form and energy showed up in the mind as rhythm in synch with nature.

Some mandalas have geometric forms that represent an aspect of/or a Deity itself. Deities are connected to us in numerous ways and can be called upon to aid when we need help. They also can be intertwined in mandalas, mandalas being a representative form, much like utilizing signs and/or symbols to represent their energies when working with occult/spiritual matters.

Mandalas can represent the Universe, the cosmic energy that flows around and through all of us, thus connecting all people and situations, much like the design of the spider web (a circle found in nature). Think of each person being on a strand of the web. When one person moves or does anything, he/she shakes the web and affects everyone. It is also the domino effect. So be conscious of what you do and only do positive. Remember, as a circle, what you do comes back to you.

When focusing on the center of the mandala, it assists you in attaining a Higher State of consciousness. The mandala evokes Cosmic Energy to be in synchronicity with you to elevate your consciousness, speed up your healing process, and can also give you Blessings.

There is Power in this form. There is serenity, peace and joy. Allow the mandala to work its magick for you. To create the harmony and prosperity in your life that you deserve to enjoy. If you feel that you do not deserve it because of something in your past, (which is anywhere from years back to a second ago-*it has passed*), then know that you are a new person with each new second and the past has no validity, no hold on you anymore. If you feel you do not deserve joy because of yourself or because of another person, it is already in the past. Focus on your future and move forward.

Take that step of Faith and know you are Divinely Guided by the hand of Divine Power. You can control and manifest what you choose in your life. Utilize the mandala to gain focus and insight.

Know that your life is under your control. Not others' control and not from your past. Your past experiences are over. Done. They no longer have a hold on you. Allow the energies of the cosmos to flow through you. Recharging you. Giving you self-empowerment, self-confidence and peace.

Go within the mandala at its center and Let Go. Surrender does not mean to give up. You are surrendering to your Higher Self to give you insight, intuition and to make the right decisions and to move you toward a better life.

Be aware of the Power that you have within you. You simply need to tune into nature's energy utilizing this tool to gain access to your Inner Gate of cosmic forces to bring peace and happiness into your life.

You are an unlimited spirit. Remember that you are energy in motion. You are a co-creator. As a co-creator, how can you be limited? You cannot be. The universe opens its arms to you, embraces you and tells you to move forward in love and joy. You are enfolded in the Love, Serenity and Peace of the cosmos. Do not limit yourself with earthly thoughts. Go forward as a spiritual warrior and create, create, create...

Pictures or other forms can be constructed to be a meditation focal point. These have symmetry and a central point. Some have cardinal points, depending on what your goal happens to be. The center is the focus for meditation purposes.

You can construct your own mandala. One of the best ways is to:

1 - First decide what type of form you feel comfortable using (draw, paint, etc.).

2 - Pick a serene place, where you will not be disturbed.

How To Eliminate Stress And Anxiety Through The Occult

3 - Next, set out all the material you will need for your endeavor.

4 - Take at least three slow, deep breaths to calm your physical body and relax all muscles.

5 - Meditate for at least 15 minutes on your Higher Self or Divine Power.

6 - Stop meditating when you feel the urge to stop (this can take a minute or hours).

7 - Pick up your tool (crayon, paint, etc.) and just draw what you FEEL.

Do NOT analyze or think about it. Just FEEL.

Remember, if you do not have an urge the first time, you are not doing this incorrectly; it simply is not the time for it to flow. Keep doing the process until you do get the feel. Also, if you made 20 mandalas in a row, it does not mean the 21st will flow. It may skip and you will not have the urge to do it. Trust your Higher Self and just relax and let it flow. Have fun with it.

How To Eliminate Stress And Anxiety Through The Occult

Maria's Bio

Maria D'Andrea, MsD, D.D., D.R.H.
is an internationally known professional psychic from Hungary. She is a published author, shaman, healing minister and officiates at ceremonies, as well as being a parapsychologist and speaker/lecturer, among other disciplines.

Maria has demonstrated psychic ability since she was a child and has been sharing her abilities, helping others make better decisions on their Path of Life for over forty years. Maria specializes in rune casting. However, she is fluent in all metaphysical, psychic and spiritual disciplines and has the ability to adjust her readings to your preference. She is well known as a spiritual leader and for teaching all aspects of the spiritual/PSI/occult fields.

Some of her other abilities include serving as a trance medium, tarot, past lives, home cleansing, dowsing, numerology, clairvoyance, business consulting, and E Mei Qi Gong.

She has been a popular radio and television guest and is the host/director/producer and script writer of her own Cablevision TV Series "The Spiritual World With Maria"; is the founder of several organizations, such as The D'Andera Institute of Esoteric Studies, the Sylvan Society, the PSI Esoteric Guild (TPEG), the Spiritrainbow Healing System, and Maria's Abundance Club (MAC).

She can be reached through her website at: www.mariadandrea.com

How To Eliminate Stress And Anxiety Through The Occult

HERE ARE THE LATEST MYSTICAL SECRETS FROM FAMED HUNGARIAN BORN PSYCHIC MARIA D'ANDREA, REVEALED IN HER NEW BOOK AND VIDEO DRAMATIZATION

COME UP TO THE "GOOD LIFE" WITH MARIA'S TOP ONE DOZEN SPELLS AND OCCULT GALLERY OF MYSTICAL AND SPIRITUAL ESSENTIALS

$24.00 + $5 S/H

Though most popularly known as the "Money Psychic," Hungarian born Maria D' Andrea is actually knowledgeable on a wide range of paranormal topics. Each week she focuses on a different topic in her widely seen TV show The Sprittual World With Maria broadcast throughout Long Island. In addition, she has given lectures and seminars on subjects that are widely diverse.

In her latest work (accompanied by a Free Bonus DVD), **MARIA D' ANDREA'S SECRET OCCULT GALLERY AND SPELL CASTING FORMULARY**, she delves into over fifty little known aspects of the occult. In addition, scattered amongst the pages are twelve of her most powerful spells that she has only shared up until now with her most privileged students.

WHY THIS OCCULT GALLERY IS IMPORTANT TO YOU— TOPICS DISCUSSED

Psychic Self-Defense · How Herbs Relate To Spiritual Work · Energy Streams: Mother Nature's Party Lines · Are You A Modern Day Prophet? Children In The Path Of Light · Manifesting Your Own Future · Utilizing The Power Of Belief · Communicating On A Psychic Level How To Be Guided By Spiritual Realms · The Secret Power Within Crystals And Candles · Journey To Another Plane Earth Changes And How They Affect You · Stones of Intrigue · Living An Alpha Reality · UFOs And Crystals Colored Lights - Effects of Being Exposed To Them · How To Use "Wind Magic" · Choices On Your Path · U.F.O.'s On The Astral Plane Identifing Forms With Power · Lucid Dreams · Ghosts Versus Spirits · Sounds Of Power · Symbolic Magick And Its Many Uses My Invisible Partners · Imagination Versus Psychic: How To Identify · Prosperity And Happiness All Yours! When To Tell You Are Guided By Spirit Beings · Out Of Body Travel Without Baggage · Telepathy: Direct Communication Ghostology: Finding Unseen Forces · The Inner Kingdom · New Age Formulary · Hobgoblins · Ghost Of The Tribes · The Tidra The Link Between Realities · Story Of The Bats · Empowerment Through The Word Influence Of UFOs On Spiritual Awareness · Dreams: Your Direct Phone Line · Dream Pillows · God's Creatures · Our Psychic Connection Psychic Rune Casting to Native Indian Crafts · Universal Lines Of Force · Tree Doctor

Revealed: Maria's Most Powerful Spells Never Published Previously! Easy To Follow And Perform Yourself

SPELL 1 - LOVE AND GOD
SPELL 2 - MANIFEST WITH THE GOD BOX
SPELL 3 - KEEPS NEGATIVITY AWAY
SPELL 4 - SEA MAGIC FOR ANY WISH
SPELL 5 - TO RELEASE ANGER
SPELL 6 - HELP FOR AN ANGELIC SPIRIT
SPELL 7 - SPELLS WITH GODDESS FREYJA
SPELL 8 - TO BRING IN LUCK
SPELL 9 - THE SPELL OF LOVE
SPELL 10 - THE WHIM OF THE GODS SPELL
SPELL 11 SUCCESS SPELL OF THE DRAGON KINGS
SPELL 12 – HAPPINESS AND HARMONY SPELL

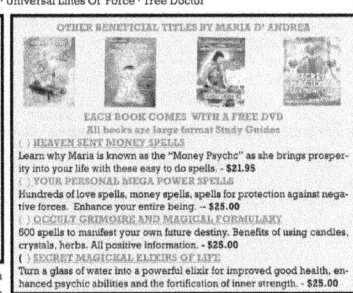

OTHER BENEFICIAL TITLES BY MARIA D' ANDREA

EACH BOOK COMES WITH A FREE DVD
All books are large format Study Guides
( ) **HEAVEN SENT MONEY SPELLS**
Learn why Maria is known as the "Money Psychic" as she brings prosperity into your life with these easy to do spells. - **$21.95**
( ) **YOUR PERSONAL MEGA POWER SPELLS**
Hundreds of love spells, money spells, spells for protection against negative forces. Enhance your entire being. -- **$25.00**
( ) **OCCULT GRIMOIRE AND MAGICAL FORMULARY**
500 spells to manifest your own future destiny. Benefits of using candles, crystals, herbs. All positive information. - **$25.00**
( ) **SECRET MAGICKAL ELIXIRS OF LIFE**
Turn a glass of water into a powerful elixir for improved good health, enhanced psychic abilities and the fortification of inner strength. - **$25.00**

HOW TO ORDER - This remarkable book and study guide with its bonus DVD is bound to enhance your being. If you are looking for success this progressive metaphysical volume is for you. And if you want a great Occult Gallery filled with a wondrous trove of information and facts, send just $24.00 + $5 S/H and request MARIA'S OCCULT GALLERY. It will be a decision you will be happy to have made.

**ALSO AVAILABLE
SPECIALLY PREPARED GEMSTONE KIT
YOU CAN USE WITH MARIA'S BOOKS & DVDS**
Contains green agate, amethyst, carnelian, citrine, hematite, green jasper, rose quartz, green quartz, clear quartz, sodalite, and tiger's eye, and a vial of lavender oil and a blue travel bag.
**ADD THIS KIT TO YOUR ORDER
FOR JUST $20.00**

**SUPER SPECIAL
5 BOOKS AND 5 DVDS IN AD $99.00 + $10 S/H
TIMOTHY G. BECKLEY · BOX 753
NEW BRUNSWICK, NJ 08903**

How To Eliminate Stress And Anxiety Through The Occult

Maria D'Andrea
Now On Dvd! A Guide To Practical Spirituality And How To Make Things Happen

MARIA D'ANDREA'S SPIRITUAL LIFE COUNSELING MINI WORKSHOPS
Effortless And Immediate Metaphysical/Psychic Techniques That Work

Let The Most Gifted Of Psychics And Spiritual Counselors Transform Your Life Into A Fountain Of Abundance

Maria D' Andrea, MsD., D.D., DRH is an internationally known professional psychic from Budapest, Hungary. Since early childhood she has demonstrated high spiritual awareness and psychic ability. Maria is a Shaman, a Metaphysician, and a Psychic Consultant

SERIES NO. ONE
3 DVD SET - $21.95

Disc # 1 – THE POWER OF PLANTING SPIRITUAL SEEDS
Maria teaches how to utilize your thoughts in a creative way so that each action becomes a most powerful tool for change. This is an excellent DVD to create positive transformations in your life.

Disc # 2 — YOU CAN LEARN TO LIVE A SHAMANIC LIFE
One of the many exercises in this DVD is trusting your first instinct. Experience a journey from beginner to master and tap into hidden knowledge so your ordinary life turns into a shamanic one.

Disc # 3 – DEVELOPING THE HEALER WITHIN YOU
Discover the hidden healer within. Here are the basic principles that allows anyone to become self empowered in the healing arts. Use for your own well being and the health of your loved ones.

SERIES NO. TWO
3 DVD SET - $21.95

Disc # 1 – ATTRACTING RELATIONSHIPS
Maria teaches how to draw more positive relationships in today's world. Learn the importance of applying ancient methods to enhance your opportunities. She also explains the power of colors, gemstones and astrological periods that are best for women and men.

Disc # 2 – SURRENDER YOURSELF TO A POSITIVE LIFE
Discover how to allow spirit to assist you in having a more exciting life. Maria teaches the importance of releasing yourself from the past, while empowering you so that you can create your future as the present moment.

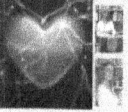

Disc # 3 – ANGELS AND THE FALL
As a Hungarian spiritual and psychic metaphysician, Maria explains the various angels and how they can assist us. She reveals the meaning and importance of shielding to assist in working with these all powerful beings. Maria shows you how to work with Archangel Ariel and Zavael with specific techniques. This DVD helps to calm the storm in your life and to create a more positive being.

VERY SPECIAL OFFER
ALL 6 DVDs JUST $39.00 + $5 S/H
ORDER FROM:
Timothy Beckley • Box 753
New Brunswick, NJ 08903
credit card order hot line:
732-602-3407

How To Eliminate Stress And Anxiety Through The Occult

IMAGINE RECEIVING MONEY JUST BY USING THE POWERS OF YOUR MIND!

Let Maria D'Andrea Tell You How To Turn Your Dreams Into Cash— And Become A Virtual Human MONEY MAGNET

Want A New Home, Or Pay Off An Existing Mortgage?

Would you like to go on an exotic "dream" vacation with someone who is sexy or your true soul mate?

Want To Sell The Items Laying Around In Your Garage Or Attic For BIG CASH! Just like on TV's *Pawn Stars*?

Interested In Picking A "Large Prize" Lottery Ticket, Or Winning At The Tables Or Slots In "Vegas?"

Tired Of Seeing Everyone Else Wearing The "Bling?" – Diamonds May Be A Girls Best Friend, But Who Cares About Anyone Else When That Fabulous Stone Could Just As Easily Be On Your Finger.

Money Is Just Another Object – You Can Learn To Collect Dollars Just As You Would Collect Anything Else As A "Hobby."

Inspired by the *Heavenly Light* here are spells that anyone can learn to execute.

Use herbs, candles and gemstones to create prosperity! Have talismans and amulets help do the work for you! Here are dozens of ways to bring Good Luck into your life!

NEW – JUST OUT!

Hop on the path to prosperity when you utilize the easy to practice empowerments in *HEAVEN SENT MONEY SPELLS – DIVINELY INSPIRED FOR YOUR WEALTH* by Maria D' Andrea for just $21.95 + $5 S/H

Born in Budapest, Maria D' Andrea, an internationally known professional psychic, occultist, hypnotist, minister, teacher and radio/television personality, for the first time passes on ancient knowledge as well as her own formulas for being FINANCIALLY SUCCESSFUL! "The forces of nature are here to be worked with in a positive way," the gifted seers has stated. "This is information that has been passed down by word of mouth from the ancient wise known by titles such as magi, shamans, priestesses, elders, and sages."

Also Available-
TRIPLE THE POWER OF THE SPELLS IN THIS BOOK WITH YOUR PERSONAL. . .

Third Pentacle of the Sun Talisman This authentic replica of an ancient talisman used by the prophets of old grants you the ability to acquire immense riches, glory and renown. Measuring 1" in diameter, this potent amulet comes on a black satin cord.

Priced to sell at $25 by itself, you may order Maria's new Heaven Sent Money Spells book and the Pentacle of the Sun Talisman for just $42.00 + $5.00 S/H

```
Order From – Timothy Beckley
Box 753 • New Brunswick, NJ 08903
Credit Card hotline 732 602-3407
PayPal MRUFO8@hotmail.com
```

How To Eliminate Stress And Anxiety Through The Occult

For our FREE catalog of books, DVD's, audio CD's and other fascinating items, send us your name and full mailing address to:

Global Communications
P.O. Box 753
New Brunswick, NJ 08903

Email: mrufo8@hotmail.com

www.conspiracyjournal.com

www.ingramcontent.com/pod-product-compliance
Lightning Source LLC
Chambersburg PA
CBHW070811100426
42742CB00012B/2325